WHEN

I SEE

THE BLOOD

Dorothy
Happy 52rd
Birthday. May
this Blood continue
Covering & Protecting
Everything in your life.
Alice

BY

DR. TIM BAGWELL

When I See the Blood
Copyright © 1998 by Tim Bagwell

All Scripture references are from the Authorized King James Version of the Bible.

McDougal Publishing is a ministry of The McDougal Foundation, Inc., a Maryland nonprofit corporation dedicated to spreading the Gospel of the Lord Jesus Christ to as many people as possible in the shortest time possible.

Published by:

McDougal Publishing
P.O. Box 3595
Hagerstown, MD 21742-3595

Visit our website: www.mcdougal.org

ISBN 1-884369-74-X

Printed in the United States of America
For Worldwide Distribution

CONTENTS

FOREWORD BY ORAL ROBERTS 5

FOREWORD BY DR. LAEL C. MELVILLE 7

INTRODUCTION 11

PART I: THE IMPORTANCE OF THE BLOOD 15
1. WHY THE BLOOD? 17
2. THE COMPOSITION OF THE BLOOD 31
3. THE BLOOD IN ANCIENT TIMES 47
4. THE BLOOD COVENANT 59

PART II: THE VIRTUES OF THE BLOOD 85
5. THE PRECIOUS BLOOD 87
6. THE JUSTIFYING BLOOD 97
7. THE ATONING BLOOD 107
8. THE RESTORING BLOOD 117
9. THE PROTECTING BLOOD 129

PART III: HOW TO ACHIEVE THE BENEFITS OF THE
BLOOD 139
10. THE AUTHORITY OF THE BLOOD 141
11. THE VOICE OF THE BLOOD 155
12. APPLYING THE BLOOD TO YOUR LIFE 167

OTHER BOOKS BY DR. TIM BAGWELL 176
ABOUT THE AUTHOR 181

FOREWORD BY ORAL ROBERTS

I'm honored to write a personal word about my dear friend, Tim Bagwell, and his terrific new book, *When I See the Blood*. A thrill went through me as I realized anew by reading Tim's precious words that I am covered by the blood of my personal Savior, Jesus Christ of Nazareth. I thought to myself: *Every believer needs this powerful reminder!*

Knowing Tim Bagwell, his lovely wife, Gayla, and his sons, Adam and Aaron, and ministering in their church in Denver has made me realize that he is a great man with an anointed church. I love those dear saints. In so many ways they reflect Tim's anointed ministry, his scholarly insights into God's Word and his passionate love and vision. His people are presently at work building a new and larger sanctuary to accomodate their exploding growth. That's what happens when a man is on fire for God.

Tim's new book inspires me and I believe it will do the same for you.

FOREWORD BY
DR. LAEL C. MELVILLE

In 1995 I contracted Lyme Disease from a tick bite. At the time, doctors could not give me the treatment of their choice because I was pregnant with my third son. When the pregnancy temporarily masked the symptoms of the disease, I thought I had escaped the terrible suffering that many who get Lyme Disease experience. After two years, however, the symptoms gradually came back with a vengeance, and I suffered terribly for several months. The fever, pain, soreness, disorientation and general fatigue associated with Lyme Disease were debilitating to the point that it became impossible for me to carry on with my daily responsibilities. Getting dressed and preparing meals for my family were difficult chores, and sometimes I could not even remember which direction the bathroom was. I was terrified! I had a successful career and a family that depended on me.

During the worst of my suffering, I would go to church and lay on the pew, but one Sunday, when I just could not get there, someone brought me a tape of a sermon on the power of the blood of Christ preached by our pastor, Dr. Tim Bagwell. I had often heard sermons that were thought-provoking and encouraging, but this sermon was more than that; it was life changing. It went straight to my heart, and, for the first time in my life, I suddenly understood the power of the blood and the gift of Christ at Calvary.

The principles put forth in that message opened my spirit for the miracle of healing to occur. As I listened to the tape, I could see Christ at Calvary, I could see His bloodstained back and the deep thorns piercing His scalp. I heard Him say that He would have stepped down out of Heaven, wrapped Himself in humanity, and suffered, bled and died — just for me. In that same instant I was healed. It happened very quickly, but I was very clear about what had happened. Further tests have shown that there is absolutely no trace of Lyme Disease in my body, and I feel great!

I also experienced a wonderful spiritual breakthrough that day. I had attended church all my life, but I never had a relationship with Christ. The anointed message of Christ's sacrifice on the cross to save us so impacted my life that I now realize that God is not a "head God" but a "heart God," that His suffering was real and still affords healing, even today. If God can get this message through to us, He can work miracles through us as well. All this revelation came to me through the tape of Pastor Bagwell's message on the blood, and I will never let go of it.

The very next day, I put on my running shoes and resumed my regular exercise regime. I felt so inspired by what God had done for me that I decided to organize a twenty-mile run to raise money for the church nursery. Many of my friends and family members joined me in the home stretch, and there, at the finish line, was Pastor Bagwell to congratulate me and help me give God glory.

Since then my story has appeared in several newspapers and magazines, on local television and on the 700 Club. To God be all the glory!

I am so pleased to be able to recommend to any who have not heard it preached the written form of this powerful message, *When I See the Blood*, and I encourage you, the reader, to let God impact your life as He has mine through this message.

And THE BLOOD shall be to you for a token upon the houses where ye are: and WHEN I SEE THE BLOOD, I WILL PASS OVER YOU, and the plague shall not be upon you to destroy you, when I smite the land of Egypt. And this day shall be unto you for a memorial; and ye shall keep it a feast to the LORD *throughout your generations; ye shall keep it a feast by an ordinance for ever.*

Exodus 12:13-14

INTRODUCTION

"When I see the blood ..."

What was it about the blood that made the difference in the lives of the oppressed Israelites in Egypt? Could this same message have any meaning for us today, in the dawning days of the twenty-first century? I am convinced that it does. I firmly believe that the key to living victoriously, to seeing God at work in our daily lives and of knowing that ours is a life of faith is recognizing and appropriating the power of the blood of Jesus Christ right here, right now. The key to walking free of the guilt that comes with sin, the key to overcoming the enemy in our lives is nothing more than the age-old message of the blood.

Why is it that these seem to be such far-off goals for Christians today? Why is it that modern-day Christians have so few mountain-top experiences? Christians of all generations have passed through times of testing and have had trials to bear, but it is clear to all those who know the Word of God that His will is for us to be able to say in the midst of every trial and test, "I am an overcomer." Many professing Christians fall far short of that mark. In fact, too many are not even able to say, "I'm going to make it."

If we look at the rising suicide rates in our nation and the world, it is alarming to note how many are giving up on life altogether, while millions of others are simply enduring, waiting for better days to come. Merely enduring life, however, is not God's best for us. Jesus Himself said:

I am come that they might have life, and that they might have it more abundantly.   John 10:10

The Word of God again and again confirms that our heavenly Father wants us to be winners and overcomers, not just "endurers" who work hard to hang on to the bitter end.

God has destined us to be *"the head and not the tail," "above only"* and not *"beneath."* He has formed us to be *"more than conquerors."* He has created us to be victorious. He has given us His sure Word:

Greater is he that is in you, than he that is in the world.   1 John 4:4

If God be for us, who can be against us?   Romans 8:31

I can do all things through Christ which strengtheneth me.   Philippians 4:13

But how can we move into a place of receiving those promises?

There is a force, a power, inside every human being who was born after the Fall — of wrath, rebellion, and disobedience. Every one of us has sinned and *"come short of the glory of God."* My father, who is now with the Lord, preached the Gospel for sixty years. My mother was saved when she was a teenager and has walked with God for almost seventy years now. This is the home into which I was born. It was a godly and Spirit-filled home. Still I sinned, and I needed Jesus. I was not automatically saved simply because my parents were saved. My sins were not washed away just because my father was a preacher and my mother was a godly woman.

Eventually, I was redeemed, but not because they were good. I was redeemed because one day I came to a place of repentance. I came to the place of admitting that no matter how many good works I might do, I could never do enough to purchase eternal salvation.

In our society, we usually try to do things in the quickest, easiest way possible. We don't like to go through a process of change. But no matter how hard we may try, there are no shortcuts in some areas. One of these is dealing with the sin nature. You cannot "cast out" the sin nature. You cannot ask an anointed servant of the Lord to "cast out" and "rebuke" the nature of sin within you. The only way that sin nature can be cast aside from your life is for you to open up to God and receive the cleansing of the blood of Christ.

No one can pray the sin away from you. The nature of sin can only be dealt with as you open the door of access to your spiritual life and allow Jesus Christ to come in and be Lord of your life. It is only as you apply His shed blood to the doorposts of your house that you can be protected, cleansed, and regenerated. Then you can truly and joyfully declare, "I am born again. I am a new creation! Old things are passed away and behold, all things are become new!"

If we can lay hold of God's intention for us, our faith can be released at a higher level. If we can know that it is not wrong for us to believe that we are winners and overcomers in life, we will begin to reach for that better thing that God has prepared. How do we accomplish that? God has given us the key, when He said, *"When I see the blood ... ."* Now, many centuries later, there is still power in the blood of the Lamb, Jesus Christ.

Let us now make a journey of discovery together, a journey from which we will surely emerge victorious through the blood of the Lamb. Let us hear God say to each of us today, *"When I see the blood, I will pass over you."*

Tim Bagwell
Denver, Colorado

Part I:

The Importance of the Blood

CHAPTER ONE

WHY THE BLOOD?

And they overcame him by THE BLOOD OF THE LAMB, and by the word of their testimony; and they loved not their lives unto the death.

Revelation 12:11

Why the blood?

Let me begin by saying that there is clearly more to having a victorious lifestyle than just possessing a lot of money or a new car. There is more to overcoming and being a winner in the game of life than being famous or even admired. Indeed, many very wealthy and famous people cannot say that they are winners. They daily lose the battle of life to drugs, to materialism or to egotism. Their marriages are failing, and their other family relationships are in shambles. They are experiencing nervous breakdowns in record numbers, and they are filled with bitterness and anger. That is not the overcoming life the Bible promises.

Overcoming implies that there is something or someone to be overcome. In the book of Revelation, John called him *"the accuser of our brethren"* (12:10).

Of this *"accuser,"* he said: *"[He] accused them before our God day and night."* This relentless demonic attack is what brings so many people to their knees in defeat. Satan is the enemy of God and the enemy of God's people, and he will not rest until he has dragged your soul into the pits of Hell.

How can we overcome this relentless *"accuser"*? One way, we are told, is through *"the word of [our] testimony."* Every believer in Christ has a personal testimony. Each one of us can say, "I was lost, but now I'm found. I know that my life, which before was worthless and vile, has been redeemed by the Lord Jesus Christ." Although there are similarities in all our testimonies, and we share many things in common, yet each testimony is unique. God has dealt with each of us in a particular way. He has removed our burdens and destroyed our yokes in ways that often amaze others. God loves each of us as individuals and deals with us as individuals. Your personal testimony, therefore, is unique and powerful. Guard it well.

There is something else that John spoke of, another weapon that we can all use for overcoming the accuser, something that moves the hand of God on our behalf. *"They overcame him by THE BLOOD OF THE LAMB."* *"The blood of the Lamb"* somehow has the power of bringing us out of darkness and into light. It has the power to release us from the bondage of Satan and to bring us into the glorious liberty of the Kingdom of God's Son. What a wonderful truth!

Tragically, much of the Church has laid aside the teachings concerning the blood of Jesus. You may have noticed that very few songs are being written about the blood of Jesus these days, very few sermons are being preached and very few books are being written on the subject. This is not a topic that is generally discussed in conferences or seminars. The blood seems to be conspicuously absent from the minds of most believers these days. The Church as a whole refuses to think about it, and this is, indeed, a tragic turn of events.

One of the reasons that less emphasis is being placed upon the blood of Jesus and its power to liberate us from sin is the negative connotation attached to the words blood and bloodshed. When we hear the word bloodshed today, we think of mass murder by some homicidal maniac or of death in a distant battlefield. When God speaks of blood, however, He is thinking of justification, of atonement, of remission, of reconciliation, of cleansing, power to overcome and of authority over all the works of the devil. These are the very things that cause us to be part of the family of God, and they come about as a result of the application of the blood of Jesus Christ in our lives. When His glory comes upon us, it comes because of the revelation people have concerning their covenant relationship and their position with Christ through His shed blood.

The devil has sought to depict the shedding of blood as something horrible and negative. He has used the violence that has swept our nation and the horror films that have become bloodier and more graphically violent as a means of making us hesitant to think and talk about the power of the blood.

In the scriptural context, the shedding of blood, in the sacrificial realm at least, was the pathway to reconciled relationship. It was the key to loosing the favor and glory of God upon a nation. We must set aside what Satan has to say about the blood and grasp a revelation of what the blood of Jesus does in our lives. Otherwise, we will be living in a position far beneath our birthright in God.

Because of the unwillingness of many to teach on this vital subject, many believers have not yet understood how to use the blood of the Lamb correctly in their lives, and millions don't even know that they can do so. A majority of Spirit-filled Christians seem to have virtually no idea of what it means to "plead the blood of Jesus." While it is true that in some circles this phrase has become part of an Evangelical or Pentecostal rhetoric with no revelation behind it, surely our failure to claim the benefits of the sacrifice of Christ's blood have contributed to our lack of power as a Body. What a sad turn of events!

In this last day and an hour, we, as members of the Body of Christ, must come to understand the full scope of the dynamic that has to do with the blood of the Lamb. We need more than rhetoric on this issue; we need a revelation from God on the subject.

Teaching on the blood seems, to many, to be too "undignified," too "unsophisticated," too "emotionalistic," and where does that leave us? Isn't that just what *the accuser*" wants? It makes him uncomfortable when we preach about the blood or sing about the blood and when we learn about the power of the blood to make us overcomers. He knows that nothing else can break the power of sin in the life of the believer, so he wants us to avoid this subject.

And why the blood? Have you ever wondered why God chose blood to be the path to reconciliation? Why didn't He choose tears? Why not prayers? The Scriptures declare the clear-cut answer to that question:

> *For the life of the flesh is in the blood: and I have given it to you upon the altar to make an atonement for your souls: for it is the blood that maketh an atonement for the soul.*   Leviticus 17:11

The life is in the blood. It is the blood — the life — that makes atonement for man's sin. It is the blood — the life — that brings cleansing to the Body of Christ. This is fitting because sin brings death (see Romans 6:23), that death can only be atoned for by life, and the life is in the blood.

The blood is what brings the covenant between God and man into effect because *"the life of the flesh is in the blood."* As the natural blood brings life to the natural body, so the blood of Christ brings life to the covenant, setting the terms of that covenant into motion. Without blood in your body there is no life, and without the shedding of the blood of Jesus, there would be no existence for the invisible and universal Body of Christ.

Why is the blood of Christ so powerful? It was the price paid for our sins, the price of our redemption. By His blood, Christ purchased man for Himself:

> *Take heed therefore unto yourselves, and to all the flock, over the which the Holy Ghost hath made you overseers, to feed the church of God, which he hath purchased with his own blood.* Acts 20:28

There is redemption and justification in His blood:

> *Being justified freely by his grace through the redemption that is in Christ Jesus: Whom God hath set forth to be a propitiation through faith in his blood, to declare his righteousness for the remission of sins that are past, through the forbearance of God.* Romans 3:24-25

> *But God commendeth his love toward us, in that, while we were yet sinners, Christ died for us.*

Why the Blood?

Much more then, being now justified by his blood, we shall be saved from wrath through him.

Romans 5:8-9

In whom we have redemption through his blood, the forgiveness of sins, according to the riches of his grace. Ephesians 1:7

We sinful mortals can hope to approach a holy God only through the intervention of the blood of Christ:

That at that time ye were without Christ, being aliens from the commonwealth of Israel, and strangers from the covenants of promise, having no hope, and without God in the world: But now in Christ Jesus ye who sometimes were far off are made nigh by the blood of Christ.

Ephesians 2:12-13

So *"the word of [our] testimony"* and *"the blood of the Lamb"* are intertwined. Our testimonies include all the things God has done for us, and the greatest of these is that He has washed us with His own blood. We are purchased by it. *"The word of [our] testimony"* contains all the elements of our covenant with God, and that covenant was ratified by the shedding of Christ's blood.

As believers, we can claim the entire Bible — Old

and New Testaments — as part of the covenant into which we have entered with our God. Both parts are needed. If it were not for the Old Testament, we would not recognize exactly Who Jesus is, particularly that He is the Messiah. In the New Testament, He fulfilled the promises made under the Old Covenant given to Abraham and to his descendants after him. When we receive Jesus as our Lord and Savior, we become heirs of God and are accounted as the offspring of Abraham:

> *For the promise, that he should be the heir of the world, was not to Abraham, or to his seed, through the law, but through the righteousness of faith. For if they which are of the law be heirs, faith is made void, and the promise made of none effect: Because the law worketh wrath: for where no law is, there is no transgression. Therefore it is of faith, that it might be by grace; to the end the promise might be sure to all the seed; not to that only which is of the law, but to that also which is of the faith of Abraham; who is the father of us all.*
>
> Romans 4:13-16

We are Abraham's heirs by faith, and we can share in the covenant God made with him. Our covenant with God is of no lesser value than that of Abraham. In fact, through the sacrifice of His blood, Christ has established a New Covenant which elevates believers to a new level.

Why the Blood?

The sacrifice of blood itself is nothing new. It was practiced in ancient times. In the New Testament, however, it is raised to a very different level. Instead of the blood of bulls and goats, we now have the sacrifice of the precious blood of the Son of God. The Bible speaks of Him as *"the Word"*:

In the beginning was the Word, and the Word was with God, and the Word was God. The same was in the beginning with God. All things were made by him; and without him was not any thing made that was made. In him was life; and the life was the light of men. John 1:1-4

And the Word was made flesh, and dwelt among us, (and we beheld his glory, the glory as of the only begotten of the Father,) full of grace and truth. John 1:14

"The Word ..." He was with the Father from the very beginning, being one with Him, living in glory with Him, yet He chose to become flesh that He might pay the ultimate price for our redemption, that He might shed His blood for us.

Joseph was not the father of Jesus, for Jesus was literally *"the Son of God."* What happened to Mary came about through the intervention of the Holy Ghost. The angel Gabriel declared:

> *The Holy Ghost shall come upon thee, and the power of the Highest shall overshadow thee: therefore also that holy thing which shall be born of thee shall be called the Son of God.*   Luke 1:35

Many have tried to minimize Jesus' divine origins to make him just a man, but it is important to believe what the Bible so emphatically shows to be true. Divine conception guaranteed that the blood flowing through Jesus' veins had no taint of human corruption. When a baby is conceived, the blood comes from the sperm, not from the egg. It is the father, not the mother, who supplies the blood to that new soul. The DNA of a man, therefore, will match, in amazing ways, the DNA of his child, and experts can identify a child's true father with total assurance by examining DNA samples.

The DNA of Jesus came not from Mary or from Joseph, but from the Holy Spirit of God. Mary was just a vessel in whose flesh the Son of the Living God would grow. In her womb, that life would take on human form:

> *Wherefore when he cometh into the world, he saith, Sacrifice and offering thou wouldest not, but a body hast thou prepared me.*
>
> Hebrews 10:5

God Himself prepared Christ's body, and there was nothing in Jesus that was not of God. There was not a single human element in His blood. It was divine and unlike any that had ever flowed through the veins and arteries of an earthling. In Jesus, there was nothing of the fallen nature inherent in all men after the Fall. He was the sinless and perfect Son of God.

Humanly speaking, everything about Jesus was like Adam before the Fall. God formed Adam thus:

> *And the LORD God formed man of the dust of the ground, and breathed into his nostrils the breath of life; and man became a living soul.*
>
> Genesis 2:7

The Hebrew word translated here as *"breath"* is *ruach,* usually translated as *"spirit."* God breathed His *"breath,"* His *"Spirit,"* into that dry dust, and man became *"a living soul."* At the time of his creation, there was nothing of a fallen nature in Adam, and, in the same way, when Jesus came forth on the Earth, there was nothing of the corruptible nature, nothing of a sinful nature, nothing of a fallen nature, in Him.

We know this to be so, for if there had been anything of sin in Jesus, He would have sinned during His time on the Earth. There has never existed a single human being since the Fall of Adam and Eve that we could point to as being sinless, but Jesus was just such a man:

For we have not an high priest which cannot be touched with the feeling of our infirmities; but was in all points tempted like as we are, yet without sin.   Hebrews 4:15

Jesus was so linked to the Father that nothing could sway Him from His appointed task of redemption. He had come to do a job, and He would do it — faithfully and fully:

But now once in the end of the world hath he appeared to put away sin by the sacrifice of himself.   Hebrews 9:26

He came to do what the Law could not do, and He would do it — without distraction.

As Jesus walked on the Earth, He ministered to the needy, healed the sick, cast out demons, and preached the Kingdom of God. He multiplied the loaves and the fishes, walked on water and raised the dead. Then, when His disciples were enjoying immensely the reaction of the multitudes to this ministry and contemplating a long and blessed service at His side, He told them one day that He would soon have to go away. They were understandably devastated by this news. What could be so important that Jesus would stop healing the sick and casting out devils and bringing new life to sinners?

Why the Blood?

He tried to explain to them that He must take His place as High Priest at the right hand of the Father. The writer of Hebrews admonished:

> *Wherefore, holy brethren, partakers of the heavenly calling, consider the Apostle and High Priest of our profession, Christ Jesus.*   Hebrews 3:1

The deeply saddened disciples were assured that they would not be left alone. Jesus promised them:

> *Nevertheless I tell you the truth; It is expedient for you that I go away: for if I go not away, the Comforter will not come unto you; but if I depart, I will send him unto you.*   John 16:7

This promise was kept. Within days after Jesus had died on Calvary, as believers gathered, the Church experienced an initial outpouring of the Holy Spirit, and common men and women were transformed into powerful instruments of God's love for the world around them. Through the miracle of Pentecost, we took on God's Spirit and became His Body. He was the Anointed One, and we have become the anointed ones. He was the Light of the world, and He has now made us to be light for the world as well.

But what is Christ's Body without His blood? If

His blood does not flow through us, we are nothing, and we can do nothing. We are overcomers only *"by the blood of the Lamb, and by the word of [our] testimony."*

Our God still says to us today, *"When I see the blood, I will pass over you."*

CHAPTER TWO

THE COMPOSITION OF THE BLOOD

> *For the life of the flesh is in THE BLOOD: and I have given it to you upon the altar to make an atonement for your souls: for it is THE BLOOD that maketh an atonement for the soul.*
>
> Leviticus 17:11

Think a moment about all that blood does for your body. Most of us have about five quarts of this miraculous liquid flowing through our veins. It is carried in a vehicle called plasma, a colorless liquid, in which are suspended various cellular elements and in which are found, in solution, a great many chemical compounds.

The first interesting thing about the blood plasma is that the fluidity of it causes it to move into every part of the human body. The blood is somehow interacting with everything that makes up your body. It interacts with every cell of every organ: your heart, your lungs, your flesh and your bones. Every dynamic of the human body is impacted by the blood.

In the same way, Christ's blood flows to all parts of His Body, of which we are a part. It touches us in every area of need, feeding, cleansing, and protecting us, doing for us spiritually what the physical blood does for the human body.

Sometimes we like to think that God is concerned only with "spiritual matters": how often we read our Bibles, whether we pray frequently, or how much we give to the church, but God does not view life quite so narrowly. He looks to all of who we are, our entire being, and His blood flows out to every part of us. His blood reaches out to our jobs, our families, our relationships, our finances, even to our specific tastes and preferences. Nothing is left untouched by the blood. As the plasma carries blood throughout our bodies, so the blood of Jesus flows in and around and through us, feeding and washing each part of us, drawing us deeper into Him.

No wonder God chose blood to be the vehicle for reconciliation! He knew that we needed every aspect of our lives to be impacted by His life-giving forces, and if we didn't get this positive spiritual flow, we could find ourselves vulnerable to the enemy.

The blood plays a part in our physical healing. The Scriptures declare:

> *But he was wounded for our transgressions, he was bruised for our iniquities: the chastisement of our peace was upon him; and with his stripes we are healed.* Isaiah 53:5

The Composition of the Blood

These *"stripes"* were the marks left behind by the cruel whip that lashed the Savior's back. His blood was shed through those stripes, and that shed blood brings healing to our physical bodies.

The blood of Jesus can likewise bring healing to our relationships. It should be obvious to us that we can never truly come into a right relationship with others if we are not in right relationship with God, and we enter into a reconciled relationship with Him by the blood:

> *But now in Christ Jesus ye who sometimes were far off are made nigh by the blood of Christ.*
>
> Ephesians 2:13

We are *"made nigh"* because the blood of Christ protects us from Satan's power. Satan comes *"to steal, kill, and destroy,"* and he is not just after our physical health; he is also out to destroy our mental health and our emotional well-being. When depression or anxiety or fear or anything else that is not of God comes against us, what can we do? We have two alternatives: we can either give in to these emotions and live under a dark cloud, trying to survive another day, or we can plead the blood of Jesus over that situation and over those emotions and gain victory over them. God promised:

> *The plague shall not be upon you to destroy you.*
>
> Exodus 12:13

When the enemy comes against you mentally or emotionally, if you have faith enough to say, "I plead the blood of the Lamb," something happens. You send the liquidity of that blood into every area of your thoughts and emotions, and God raises up a standard against the enemy.

This is not simply the power of positive thinking, nor is it some other mental therapy or discipline. It is the outworking of the understanding that your hedge, your shield, your protection, and your covering is not in anything you do or could do in the natural. You must, by faith, understand and receive the truth that the precious blood of Christ covers every aspect of your life, bringing His protection, His covering, His very life to you. Thank God for the blood!

The red blood cells carried by the plasma are disc-shaped cells containing a substance called hemoglobin, an iron compound with an affinity for oxygen. These red blood cells deliver digested food molecules and oxygen to every part of the body. They also pick up waste carbon dioxide from the body cells and carry it back to the lungs to be expelled from the body. This amazing round trip takes about twenty seconds.

Just as those red blood cells distribute food where it is needed throughout the body, Christ's blood provides our spiritual food. It is the nourishment of the Word of God:

The Composition of the Blood

And I went unto the angel, and said unto him, Give me the little book. And he said unto me, Take it, and eat it up; and it shall make thy belly bitter, but it shall be in thy mouth sweet as honey. And I took the little book out of the angel's hand, and ate it up; and it was in my mouth sweet as honey: and as soon as I had eaten it, my belly was bitter.

Revelation 10:9-10

Our food is the Word of God, the Bible, and it is the blood that has made the New Covenant available to us. Like John, we are to consume the Word. This is the fuel we need if we are to become strong in the Lord. We grow and are strengthened by what we eat. David said:

Thou preparest a table before me in the presence of mine enemies.

Psalm 23:5

God has prepared a table for each of us, He has set it before us. We may eat of it when things are going well, and also when the enemy threatens, for He has prepared it for us *"in the presence of [our] enemies."* He invites us to partake of the Word, which is our feast.

God's Word does not provide enough to merely sustain us. As with all gifts of the Father, there is an overflowing abundance to be found by those who will seek. As we seek, we shall find, and as we eat the Word, we shall be made strong in Christ.

On the night He was betrayed, Jesus shared the emblems of the New Covenant with His closest disciples. He let them know that the entire New Covenant rests upon His blood:

> *Likewise also the cup after supper, saying, This cup is the new testament in my blood, which is shed for you.* Luke 22:20

Because of Christ's blood, the New Covenant is made available to all who believe. We cannot access the covenant without the blood. We cannot partake of the covenant without the red blood cells that bring us the food of the Word. As we eat the Word, all that we need for life in Christ is imparted to us. What a wonderful blessing!

Just as the red blood cells carry off the waste from the body, even so the same Word that brings strength and life to us also discerns the good from the bad in our lives. It brings conviction for sin, rebellion, and wrath. In this way, it is able to remove the debris, the garbage, from our lives:

> *The blood of Jesus Christ his Son cleanseth us from all sin.* 1 John 1:7

> *Unto him that loved us, and washed us from our sins in his own blood.* Revelation 1:5

The blood of Christ is a cleansing blood, and it washes away our sins. Never underestimate that power.

The white blood cells found in human blood are also important. These cells attack any germs that invade the body, surrounding them and swallowing them. Together with the antibodies found in blood, they form the body's immune system.

The white blood cells are not nearly as predominant as the red blood cells are. Because it is so important to get the fuel in and the garbage out, human blood normally contains four to five million red blood cells per cubic millimeter. In contrast, there are only four to seven thousand white blood cells per cubic millimeter. When infection enters into the body, however, an interesting thing happens. Suddenly the number of white blood cells doubles and then triples. These cells are intent upon engulfing infection and destroying it before it can cause serious damage to the body.

What does this have to do with the Christian life? The infection that threatens to destroy our lives comes from the whispered lies of the enemy, from seemingly minor sins or from the unkind thoughts or words that try to take root in us and grow. The enemy continually tries to contaminate our lives, seeking to bring in things that are neither clean nor righteous. He hopes to destroy the very essence of who we can be in God. But just as the white blood cells in your physical bloodstream rise up to fight infection, so the power of the Spirit of God rises inside you to fight off the enemy:

> *When the enemy shall come in like a flood, the Spirit of the Lord shall lift up a standard against him.*   Isaiah 59:19

Jewish rabbis translated this verse a little differently:

> *When the enemy shall come in, like a flood the Spirit of the Lord shall lift up a standard against him.*

Simply moving a comma brings a new meaning to this verse. The rabbis saw the Lord as the flood that would overcome the enemy, and He will do it every time if we believe Him for it.

Many Christians find that once they come to the Lord, they cannot sin as they once did. For one thing, the desire to sin is greatly reduced. Secondly, when a believer does sin, the spiritual white blood cell count shoots up to counteract that sin before it can take root and threaten our spiritual lives.

Many diseases can be detected in the body through a simple blood test. When blood is examined, an unusually high white cell count indicates that some infection is present. When the Lord examines us and sees the high spiritual white blood cell count, He knows that something is wrong internally. We may try to deny that anything is amiss, but we cannot hide anything from God. He knows us better than we know ourselves, and we must respond quickly and willingly to the convicting power of His Spirit. He is not trying to hurt or embarrass us; He is trying to stop the infection that is invading our souls before it can become serious enough to destroy us.

God has a purpose for your life, and once you have entered into a relationship with Him, He will never leave you defenseless. When anything threatens your spiritual life, He will multiply His presence in your life and attack that which threatens to do you harm.

When the prodigal son became spiritually ill, he said to his father, "Give me all my inheritance right now." After he had obtained his inheritance, he went out and quickly spent it all in *"riotous living."* This brought his life to ruin, and he ended up in a pigpen. Even there, however, God's presence was fighting for him.

Many Christians have had pigpen experiences and lived to tell it. When you stubbornly persist in having your own way, there is little that God can do to help you, but when you wind up in a pigpen, somehow you come to your senses and realize what a terrible mistake you have made. As a raging infection was flowing through your spirit man, you probably even said angry things about God. You may have said, "I don't want to serve God anymore. I will never go to church again. I was hurt too many times."

The Holy Ghost understands all your hurts and is determined to convict you of your waywardness and to bring you back to Father's house. He will not leave you, even in the pigpen of life. The prodigal son *"came to himself"*:

> *And when he came to himself, he said, How many hired servants of my father's have bread enough and to spare, and I perish with hunger! I will arise and go to my father, and will say unto him, Father, I have sinned against heaven, and before thee.*
>
> Luke 15:17-18

The white blood cells had their effect! The sinner returned to the father with repentance, and so may we.

We need to "come to" ourselves. We need to realize who we are in God, that He does not desire that we live defeated lives, and that we are free and can live a life of overcoming.

Sometimes our struggles come through our own sins, but sometimes they come through an accusation, a discouraging word, a relational or financial problem. A germ has been loosed within us, and we begin to weaken. Even though food is coming in and waste is going out, something is waging war with our spirits. We may say, "God doesn't care anymore. God isn't hearing my prayer anymore," and allow that intruding element to go through our vessel. But the Holy Spirit is working on our behalf, even if we have not asked Him specifically to do it. Just like the white blood cells in our bloodstream that are working, even when we don't realize that anything is wrong, God has not left us defenseless.

This explains why the Holy Ghost sometimes works on areas of our lives that we didn't even know needed help, convicting us of things that we didn't even realize were the cause of the dryness of our spirits. Whether we are conscious of His actions or not, He is diagnosing the infection, attacking it, and destroy anything that threatens to take us out of fellowship with God.

There are many different kinds of infections that Satan tries to inject into our walk with God, but every time we plead the blood of Christ and look to Calvary, any infection at all is diagnosed, attacked, and destroyed. We don't have to understand it. If we are feeling ill, we just need to say, "God, I'm sick. Please help me."

In addition to the plasma and the red and white blood cells, there is another ingredient that makes up our blood. These are the antibodies that work with the white blood cells in fighting infection.

While white blood cells fight infections after they

occur, antibodies are in the blood to prevent infection. This is often spoken of as "resistance." If someone has worked too hard for too long — burning the candle at both ends, so to speak — then his resistance is lowered and he may be more apt to lose the battle to an infection and become ill. When the physical body is overworked and doesn't get enough rest, the supply of antibodies that is normally found in the bloodstream is exhausted. Consequently, there are not enough of them present to prevent infection.

If we had no antibodies in our bloodstream, we would perish. We see this in AIDS victims. Their bodies lack the ability to resist infection, and they contract many different sicknesses. Without enough antibodies in our bloodstream, we are susceptible to any and every germ.

Once we have been infected with certain illnesses, antibodies are built up against those illnesses, and we will never get them again. This includes such diseases as smallpox, chicken pox, scarlet fever and measles. You may later be around those who are sick with one of these diseases, but if you have had it, you don't worry about it. You are immune to that disease. Learning to plead the blood of Jesus guards you against the repetition of sin.

With some sicknesses, the immunity you build up may not protect you totally the next time you are subject to that germ, and you may contract the disease again. This time, however, it will be a light case, and you will get over it quicker and more easily than you expected. Each attack that is resisted builds a higher level of immunity until the next time the enemy brings that particular temptation before you — the liquor or the anger or the immoral temptation — you will find yourself saying, "How could I commit this sin against my God?" and you will turn from it and walk away.

Often, after you have walked with the Lord for a time, you will notice that you no longer have a battle with certain temptations that assailed you before. When this happens you become a very effective minister to others. You can be in the same room all day with a very spiritually sick person, praying with them, talking with them, ministering to them, and you will have no fear of infection.

This is not a psychological victory. It can only happen when the blood is properly applied to your heart and life. When the blood has been applied, you can deal with things you were never able to deal with before. You can resist things you could not resist before. You can help people overcome sins that once drug you down.

The Apostle Paul had a battle that we have never come to fully understand. Three times he prayed that the thing that tormented him might be lifted. God's answer to him is interesting:

And he said unto me, My grace is sufficient for thee: for my strength is made perfect in weakness. Most gladly therefore will I rather glory in my infirmities, that the power of Christ may rest upon me. 2 Corinthians 12:9

God is able to do for you what you cannot do for yourself. Let the grace of God be loosed in your life through the application of the blood. God wants to build up your spiritual immune system until nothing can infect you.

This may not make any sense to you, but I imagine that it also did not make sense to Rahab to place a scarlet thread (which spoke of the blood) in her window. When the city of Jericho started shaking, however, and everything around her crumbled, she was glad she had obeyed.

A feeling of remorse for sin is not enough; much more is needed. The main difference between a sinner and a saint is that the saint hates his sin and pleads the blood of Christ against it, whereas the sinner loves his sin and goes back to it again and again. The saint is like a sheep who has fallen into a mud hole. He is not happy there and calls for the shepherd to come and get him out. Once he has fallen into the same mud hole a few times, he learns to avoid it.

The sinner, on the other hand, is like a pig. He loves the mud and goes in search of it. When he finds a convenient slime pit he slides into it with great glee and objects loudly if someone tries to get him out.

Christians may not be perfect, but they know the source of true perfection:

> *But if we walk in the light, as he is in the light, we have fellowship one with another, and the blood of Jesus Christ his Son cleanseth us from all sin. If we say that we have no sin, we deceive ourselves, and the truth is not in us. If we confess our sins, he is faithful and just to forgive us our sins, and to cleanse us from all unrighteousness.*
>
> 1 John 1:7-9

The moment contamination tries to enter your life, something within you begins to resist. God wants to build up within each of us an immunity to sin that will protect us in the days ahead.

Why did God choose blood as the path to reconciliation? Because it touches every dimension of every fiber of our being: body, soul, and spirit; because it feeds us and cleanses us; because it fights against infection; and because it can build up an immunity in our spirits to all that would do us harm in the future. Let us lay hold of the power of the blood of the Lamb and become *"more than conquerors through Him who loved us."*

Hear the Lord speaking to you again today. He is saying, *"When I see the blood, I will pass over you."*

CHAPTER THREE

THE BLOOD IN ANCIENT TIMES

Unto Adam also and to his wife did the LORD God make COATS OF SKINS, and clothed them.

Genesis 3:21

Blood has played a part in the plan of redemption from the time man first fell into sin. After Adam and Eve had sinned, God clothed them with the skins of animals. Those skins represented the sacrifice of the animals given for their redemption. The blood of those animals had been shed to appease the wrath of God and to bring Adam and Eve into a reconciled relationship with Him.

The Old Testament sacrificial system was never based on the flesh of animals, but on their blood. When the meat of certain sacrifices was burned and offered up to God, the aroma that arose from that burning was a memorial of the blood that had been shed.

Before the Fall, Adam and Eve lived in a beautiful and spacious garden. It was a wonderful place, specially prepared for them, where they could live in intimate fellowship with one another and with their Creator. In that garden they enjoyed an intimacy with God that men have sought after ever since.

Unfortunately, no matter how often the story is retold, the ending is always the same. Although they were warned by God not to eat of the fruit of *"the tree of the knowledge of good and evil,"* Adam and Eve yielded to the temptation of the serpent rather than obey the Lord's warning. As a result, they had to suffer the consequences. No sooner had both of them eaten the fruit of the tree than the negative results of their actions became evident:

> *The eyes of them both were opened, and they knew that they were naked.*   Genesis 3:7

Adam and Eve knew immediately that the relationship between them and their Creator had been violated. They also understood for the first time that they were unclothed. What exactly did that mean? We usually think of nakedness as being nudity, but the nakedness Adam and Eve experienced was beyond mere nudity. They had been clothed from the beginning of their existence with the glory of God, but when sin came in, it did what sin always does: it stripped them of the glory that had been their covering.

When the eyes of the first man and woman were

opened, what they experienced was not mere nudity, but the shock of being left with nothing but flesh. Sin had ruthlessly ripped the clothing of the glory of God from Adam and Eve, and for the first time in their existence, they looked at one another, and saw nothing but flesh. The former glory, the former power and the former authority were all gone. They were *"naked"* in the most awful sense. Spiritual nakedness is much more shocking than physical nudity.

There are a lot of naked Christians running around these days. They were once blood-bought children of God, but they have chosen to step outside of their covenant relationship with Him. It is no surprise to hear them say, "I don't feel what I used to. I no longer know the warmth and peace I once felt." Their garment of covering has been removed because they have willingly thrown aside the glory of the Lord.

In reality, when each of us stands before God, we are naked. We have nothing with which to cover ourselves. All the stains of sin upon our lives — the vulgarity, the vileness, the wrath, the immorality, and the rebellion — are there in plain view. There is nothing we can do to justify ourselves and reconcile ourselves with God. If we will just plead the blood of the Lamb, however, He will wash away all our sins and clothe us in His righteousness.

Adam and Eve saw their nakedness immediately

and knew that they must do something to cover themselves again. They did the best they could:

> *And they sewed fig leaves together, and made themselves aprons.*   Genesis 3:7

Adam and Eve tried desperately to cover their sin. They frantically tried to hide their shame. They even thought they might be able to hide themselves from the presence of God. The response of sinners has not changed much over the centuries, I'm afraid.

When God came down to deal with the situation, however, nothing was hidden. He knew everything that had occurred. He spoke to each of them in turn — the man, the woman and the serpent — and told them what the serious, long-term consequences of their actions would be. He did not, however, leave Adam and Eve alone in that sad state of loss. He declared the coming of the Messiah, a Redeemer for all mankind, One who, through the sacrifice of His own life, would ransom man from his sinfulness.

Then God did something that had never been done before. He made *"coats of skins, and clothed them."* Adam and Eve had tried to cover themselves, but they could not. Their feeble attempts at righting the wrongs they had done were unacceptable to God, and they quickly learned that they could not restore right relationship with the Creator through the works of the flesh. Their fig-leaf aprons could not cover what sin had exposed.

There is no way the first man and woman could have anticipated what God would do next. No blood sacrifice had ever been given until that time, for there had been no need of it. Now God caused some animals to die and their blood to be spilled, and this act brought reconciliation. Man could again approach a holy God.

Although this was the first time in human history that such a sacrifice had been made, it had to be done, for Adam and Eve had sinned, and atonement was necessary. The *"coats"* they wore from that day foreword would be for symbols to them, a testimony. Each time either of the two looked at the other, they would see those skins, remember that they had sinned, and that a blood sacrifice had been required to remove their shame and to cover them again.

Adam and Eve had to put aside the aprons they had made for themselves of fig leaves. Fig leaves were not effective for covering sin. Only blood could do that. When God put those coats on Adam and Eve, He sent a message to them, to the heavenly angels, and to the devil and his angels: "When I require a blood sacrifice, it has a purpose. It is to cover My people and restore their dignity and glory!"

This blood-based relationship was not just for Adam and Eve. It was for their children and grandchildren and all succeeding generations. Cain and

Abel, the first two sons, had to face their own test in this regard:

> *And in process of time it came to pass, that Cain brought of the fruit of the ground an offering unto the LORD. And Abel, he also brought of the firstlings of his flock and of the fat thereof. And the LORD had respect unto Abel and to his offering: But unto Cain and to his offering he had not respect. And Cain was very wroth, and his countenance fell.* Genesis 4:3-5

Some have wondered why God, who is *"no respecter of persons,"* would accept the offering of one son and reject the offering of the other. Abel's offering was from his animals. It was a blood offering. When the Lord smelled the smoke of that offering, He knew that blood had been shed as He had ordained, and He blessed Abel.

Cain, however, tended the fields and believed that his produce was just as good an offering to God as Abel's lambs. God, however, was not dealing with the two men on the basis of their chosen vocations; He was dealing with them on the basis of His covenant. If relationship was to be restored, if an offering was to be acceptable, it had to be an offering of life, an offering of blood.

God has not changed through the ages. He still has no respect for a bloodless offering for sin today.

The teachings that go forth today which seek to dispense with the blood will not be respected by God. There will be no favor upon such theologies or upon those churches that embrace them. God respects only the covenant He made with man at the beginning.

Abel remembered that covenant and gave an offering acceptable to God, but Cain violated the covenant, believing that the blood aspect of it was unimportant. His actions were deliberate and not done in ignorance, for Adam and Eve had taught their sons well. If they had not, God would not have held Cain accountable. Cain knew what he was doing and carefully chose the path he would follow. He thought that he could present a bloodless sacrifice, a sacrifice of convenience. He believed that the works of his hands would be enough and was determined to rely on the flesh.

When Cain's offering was rejected, he compounded his problem by reacting badly. Instead of repenting of his willfulness and doing the thing that would have restored him to God, he became angry — with God and with his brother:

> *And the Lord said unto Cain, Why art thou wroth? and why is thy countenance fallen? If thou doest well, shalt thou not be accepted? and if thou doest not well, sin lieth at the door.*
>
> Genesis 4:6-7

What God was saying is quite simple. "If you would do what I told you to do, I would accept your sacrifice." It seems that no matter how clearly God makes His covenants known, there is always someone who wants to put fruit on the altar when He is asking for blood. There is always someone trying to sew a fig-leaf apron together, saying, "This will surely get the job done." How vain it is to imagine that our little ideas or philosophies will cover our sins! Yet we keep on sewing our aprons and holding them up to God, saying, "Look, God, I made it myself! You'll surely have to accept it."

But God replies, "No, I cannot accept it. It must be done My way."

God was not showing favoritism to Abel because He loved him any more than He did Cain. He was showing him favor because Abel had done what God told him to do. God had a good reason for rejecting Cain's sacrifice. He accepts nothing but the blood as a sacrifice for sins. When He smelled the burning of the flesh upon the altar, He knew that blood had been spilled. When He smelled the burning of Cain's fruits, however, He knew that no blood had been spilled, and He therefore rejected the sacrifice. It could be no other way.

Cain, however, was beyond reasoning. He reacted very violently to his humiliation:

And Cain talked with Abel his brother: and it came

*to pass, when they were in the field, that Cain
rose up against Abel his brother, and slew him.*

Genesis 4:8

Cain had room for repentance. God had told him
what to do to gain acceptance, but it was all too
much for his stubborn pride. If he wanted to sacrifice an animal of the flocks, he would have to go to
his brother to get it, since Abel was in charge of the
herds. Cain would have to admit to his brother that
he (Abel) had been right and that he (Cain) had been
wrong. That, of course, is exactly what he should
have done, but he just could not bring himself to do
it. Instead, he was furious with his brother, and
when the opportunity presented itself, he killed him.

There is a significant lesson here for us today. The
religious system, a self-perpetuating system that
neither feels a need for God nor loves Him and
which tries to do everything in the flesh, often per-
secutes those who embrace God's pattern. Cain
would not submit to the plan and purpose of God
himself, so he lashed out at Abel who had done nothing wrong. The spirit of the adversary that was
working within Cain caused him to resist and rebel
against the principles of covenant that had been
passed on to him by his father. He became angry
because he could not have his own way and because
he was not willing to do things God's way. When
any person is determined to do things God's way,

he or she will be opposed and persecuted by those who want God to accept their fruit offerings or their fig-leaf aprons and are angry when He doesn't. These spiritual attacks are often unexpected and alarming, so get ready for them. There is a price to be paid if you are to stay in the favor of God.

Far too many in the Church today try to find substitutes for the supernatural remedies of God. They want to find an easier, more palatable, more politically-correct means than the blood covenant which God has provided. The problem is that God will not accept it. Men might be persuaded, but God does not change His mind. There can be no substitution of man's ways for God's ways. He simply will not permit it.

Those who are of the same religious system as Cain refuse to revere the blood, setting it aside as something not to be discussed. The spirit of Cain still struggles against the spirit of righteous Abel, and that willful spirit is still abroad in the Earth. Motivated by the devil, working in obstinate self-righteousness, this spirit is out to destroy the Kingdom of God and to rob His blessing from those who are walking in blood covenant with Christ.

Why should we keep working on our aprons, when we can be wearing *"the word of [our] testimony"*? Why should we continue to rely on the works of our hands, the fruits of our labor, when we can be covered by the blood of the spotless Lamb? It doesn't make sense.

The Blood in Ancient Times

The hymn writer understood this truth when he penned:

What can wash away my sin?
Nothing but the blood of Jesus;
What can make me whole again?
Nothing but the blood of Jesus.

Oh! precious is the flow
That makes me white as snow;
No other fount I know,
Nothing but the blood of Jesus.

Robert Lowry

That blood contains no human frailty or ineptitude. It is pure and unadulterated, precious and perfect, and acceptable in the eyes of the Father. When we plead the blood of Jesus, therefore, the Father looks not at us, with our human failings, but to the blood of His own dear Son. He says, as in days of old, *"When I see the blood, I will pass over you."*

CHAPTER FOUR

THE BLOOD COVENANT

And God said unto Abraham, Thou shalt keep my covenant therefore, thou, and thy seed after thee in their generations.   Genesis 17:9

The Lord Jesus the same night in which he was betrayed took bread: And when he had given thanks, he brake it, and said, Take, eat: this is my body, which is broken for you: this do in remembrance of me. After the same manner also he took the cup, when he had supped, saying, This cup is the new testament IN MY BLOOD: this do ye, as oft as ye drink it, in remembrance of me. For as often as ye eat this bread, and drink this cup, ye do show the Lord's death till he come.
1 Corinthians 11:23-26

If you are tired and exhausted from trying to work your way into blessing, then I have good news for you: You can enter into God's rest. God's blessing comes because of the covenant, not because of your works. If you are struggling in your spiritual walk, trying to understand the things of the Kingdom on an intellectual basis alone, then I have good news for you: You can draw on your spirit to make a demand on what is available to you in the Kingdom through the sacrifice of Jesus Christ. You can have a revelation of the covenant, and when God grants you that revelation, it will change the way you live your life in Him.

God cut the blood covenant with Abraham thousands of years ago, but that covenant is still in effect for those of us who are believers today. Paul wrote:

> *Know ye therefore that they which are of faith, the same are the children of Abraham.*
>
> Galatians 3:7

When God brought us out of darkness into His wonderful light, He brought us into a place of covenant with Him through the blessing of Abraham. What exactly was the blessing spoken to Abraham? Let us look to the account found in the book of Genesis:

> *And the LORD said unto Abram, after that Lot was separated from him, Lift up now thine eyes, and look from the place where thou art northward, and southward, and eastward, and westward: For all the land which thou seest, to thee will I give it, and to thy seed for ever. And I will make thy seed as the dust of the earth: so that if a man can*

number the dust of the earth, then shall thy seed also be numbered. Arise, walk through the land in the length of it and in the breadth of it; for I will give it unto thee. Genesis 13:14-17

"For all the land which thou seest, to thee will I give it, and to thy seed forever." Please notice that the verb form used in this promise is in the future tense. This means that God was making a promise that was yet to be fulfilled. He was prophetically promising to do certain things for Abram and for his seed. This was not the entire covenant. In fact, although a promise was made, this was not really a covenant at all. I will show you what I mean by that as we continue to examine the story of Abram.

Genesis 14 contains an account of war between two confederacies of kings. The group that won then raided the land of the other group, capturing the remaining people and collecting their belongings as spoils. Lot, Abram's nephew, was living in Sodom at the time, and since Sodom was among the dominions of those who had lost the war, he and his family and possessions were taken. One of his servants escaped and ran to tell Abram what was happening.

Abram gathered his men and pursued the armies of the kings, bringing back both the people and their possessions. The king of Sodom, in gratitude, came to meet Abram at Shaveh to thank him, but there was another man present, a man who has remained something of a mystery to Bible readers. His name was Melchizedek:

> *And Melchizedek king of Salem brought forth bread and wine: and he was the priest of the most high God. And he blessed him, and said, Blessed be Abram of the most high God, possessor of heaven and earth: And blessed be the most high God, which hath delivered thine enemies into thy hand. And he gave him tithes of all.*
>
> Genesis 14:18-20

Just who was Melchizedek? The Bible tells us very little about him, but it does say that he was *"the priest of the most high God."* In other words, Melchizedek was a mediator between God and man.

Some interesting things took place between this priest and the returning warrior. First, bread and wine were *"brought forth."* This was not simply an act of hospitality. The ancients used these elements as tokens of covenant. This was not true only of the Hebrews. The tradition went back much further than them. In earliest times, when the concept of covenant was being established, bread and wine were established as tokens or symbols of covenant.

This should sound very familiar to Christian believers, for at the Last Supper, Christ used these very symbols.

Christ was presenting the tokens that would ratify a new covenant, one that would come into effect within a very few hours, and He used the same ancient symbols. Bread and wine, therefore, remind us of the sacrifice and suffering of Jesus Christ. They remind us of the giving of His body, of the shedding of His blood, and of our reconciliation with the Father through that blood.

It was with these same symbols that Melchizedek, *"the priest of the most high God,"* began the preliminaries for the establishment of a covenant relationship between God and Abram.

Abram's response was to give Melchizedek a tithe of the spoil he had recovered from the other kings. This represents an exchange of gifts, and what Melchizedek brought to the table is not certain. It may have been simply the bread and wine itself, or it may have been his affirmation of God's promise to give Abram the land. What gift could be more valuable?

Tithing, then, is an ancient custom, dating from before the time the Law was given to Moses. It is not related to the Levitical priesthood, but to the law of faith, the priesthood of Jesus Christ. Tithing is not just to be done at the whim of those who have been blessed by God. It has a sacred aspect that few comprehend. It is a covenant gift, and we get much in exchange for our offering of love to God.

Abraham lived long before the Law was given,

and he lived under a sacred blood covenant with the Father. He had been chosen by God for this honor. When we think of the Old Testament, or Old Covenant, we usually think of the time following Moses and the giving of the Law on Mt. Sinai, but the promises of God go back much further, to this man of faith, living under blood covenant. The relationship of Abraham with the Father was not established through the keeping of the Law, but through the shedding of blood. That covenant was eternal and, therefore, is still in effect today.

Melchizedek, as the intermediary between the throne of God and Earth, was the priest who received the tithe. Abraham, as the giver of the tithe, the one who entered into covenant with God, became the father of the righteous. Melchizedek brought the bread and the wine, and Abram brought the tithe.

Does all this have something to do with us? Absolutely! The Scriptures speak of Jesus, our High Priest, as being *"a priest after the order of Melchizedek"*:

The LORD hath sworn, and will not repent, Thou art a priest for ever after the order of Melchizedek.
Psalm 110:4

As he saith also in another place, Thou art a priest for ever after the order of Melchisedec.
Hebrews 5:6
(See also Hebrews 6:20, 7:1, 10, 11, 15, 17 and 21)

The act of exchange between Abram and Melchizedek had the sweet fragrance of the prophetic promise of the coming New Testament.

Very soon, God dealt more intimately with Abram:

And he brought him forth abroad, and said, Look now toward heaven, and tell the stars, if thou be able to number them: and he said unto him, So shall thy seed be. And he believed in the LORD; and he counted it to him for righteousness.

Genesis 15:5-6

Abram *"believed in the Lord."* This is not speaking of mental assent. Abram heard what the Lord spoke, and then he made an unqualified commitment of himself — all that he was, all that he had, and all he would ever be. This unqualified commitment was made with no strings attached. From that day, everything Abram had belonged to the One with whom he had covenanted.

In a very sacred moment, Abram took a leap of faith, but he did have some doubts. He said to God, "You made me a promise. You told me that my seed would be *'as the stars of the sky and the sand of the sea,'* that I would be *'the father of a great nation.'* Still, I am childless. How can I be what You have said I would be without a child?"

Abram was not like some. He could have said,

"God, You have apparently forgotten Your promise, so why should I trust You with all that I am and all that I have?" Something told him that God was worthy of his trust, and he chose to believe Him — despite the contrary circumstances. Something happened in Abram's spirit, and he became willing to make an unqualified commitment to God — even though his circumstances seem to say that what God had promised was unlikely to come to pass. This leap of faith changed everything for Abram. It was *"imputed to him for righteousness"*:

> *He staggered not at the promise of God through unbelief; but was strong in faith, giving glory to God; And being fully persuaded that, what he had promised, he was able also to perform. And therefore it was imputed to him for righteousness.*
>
> Romans 4:20-22

Righteousness means being in "right standing with God." When Abram believed, his position changed. He was counted righteous. That doesn't mean that he was holy, not in any legalistic way, at least. He was in right standing. He was in a correct position with God.

Had Abram done something to earn this change of position before God? Not at all! It was a gift from his heavenly Father, and he received it because he was willing to believe God's promises and to make an unqualified commitment of everything that he was and would ever be and everything that he had and would ever have.

When you begin to truly believe God, when you begin to trust Him without reservation, you hang everything on the cross with Him, and you say, "Lord, I am Yours. Everything I have and everything I am is Yours. I surrender to Your Lordship. I have come to realize that You know what is best for me, better than I know it myself." That is the relationship with Jehovah God into which Abram was entering — by faith:

> *And he said unto him, I am the LORD that brought thee out of Ur of the Chaldees, to give thee this land to inherit it. And he said, Lord GOD, whereby shall I know that I shall inherit it? And he said unto him, Take me an heifer of three years old, and a she goat of three years old, and a ram of three years old, and a turtledove, and a young pigeon. And he took unto him all these, and divided them in the midst, and laid each piece one against another: but the birds divided he not.*
>
> Genesis 15:7-10

Abram had, in effect, said to God, "Lord, I have given You my all. I have given You my life and my future. I have made an unqualified commitment of myself to You. But how do I know that I will inherit the things You have promised?"

God answered, *"Take me an heifer of three years old."* This may not seem very significant to us, but it was for Abram. A three-year-old heifer or ram or goat is at the prime of its existence. It has reached maturity. If the animal is allowed to grow older, it may, at some point, become diseased or worn. A three-year-old is at its best. Abraham was not to fear to commit his very best to God. He would lose nothing in the transaction.

When Abram asked, "What is the sign that You are going to do this for me?" the answer he received from God was, in essence, "Shed blood."

The process God described for the sacrifice is typical of actions taken by parties interested in making covenant with each other in those days. A sacrificial animal was divided in half, and the two pieces were laid on the ground. The two parties then walked around and between the sacrifice, and as they did, they spoke the covenantal terms and spoke blessings upon each other. When Abram did this, he was declaring that he was entering into a covenant with Jehovah God. When God did it, he was declaring that He was entering into covenant with Abram.

It is interesting to note that the sacrifices Abram was asked to provide would later be proscribed for the entire nation of Israel in the Law. Because the people were of varying economic levels, some could afford to offer a heifer, while others could sacrifice a goat or a ram. The poorest could only afford a pigeon, but that was also acceptable. These offerings, the tokens of covenant that Abram and his heirs brought before the Lord, speak to all mankind — from the poorest beggar to the richest king. God has established a covenant with all the heirs of Abram — rich and poor alike. None are excluded.

Abram had to protect his sacrifice:

> *And when the fowls came down upon the carcases, Abram drove them away.*   Genesis 15:11

Abram kept a watch over his sacrifices because he didn't want birds to eat them. If just one bird had threatened his sacrifice, it would not have been a great problem for the man of faith. It appears, however, that there were a great number of birds, and they seemed to be large scavengers. Scavengers are difficult to get rid of. They may be frightened off for the moment, but they hover nearby and, just as soon as they see an opening, they come right back and continue their feast.

When we make a covenant with God, there will always be vultures trying to feed on that covenant sacrifice. There will always be scavengers seeking to desecrate our covenant and its symbols. Doubters, people of unbelief, and lying spirits and the like will try to come in and persuade you that your covenant cannot be carried out or that you are deluding yourself in believing that God even cares to make a permanent covenant with you. In every way he can, Satan will make it difficult for you to carry through with the promises you have made to God.

How should you respond? Have the spirit of Abram, the father of the righteous. He did not stop to speak with the fowl, nor to try to strike some bargain with them. He simply *"drove them away."* He cried out within his spirit and said, "I will not let anything come between me and my God, I will not let anything touch my covenant with Jehovah. I will fight this thing all day and all night if necessary. I will fight for the rest of my life if necessary, but these vultures will not devour the tokens of covenant which stand between God and me!" He meant it, and God honored his stand:

> *And it came to pass, that, when the sun went down, and it was dark, behold a smoking furnace, and a burning lamp that passed between those pieces. In the same day the LORD made a covenant with Abram, saying, Unto thy seed have I given this land.* Genesis 15:17-18

Until now, God had been speaking in the future, *"I will give ... ,"* but now that was all changed. Now God was saying, *"I have given ... ."* What brought about this dramatic change? The covenant had been ratified. The blood had been shed, and both parties had passed among the emblems of covenant. The covenant was now in effect. The promises to Abraham were no longer future. They had become present realities in Abram's life.

You may be looking at your own life and wondering, "Lord, when will these things that You have spoken come to pass in my life? When will I receive all that I have heard You speak to me? When will the prophetic words spoken over me become reality?"

The Lord's reply to you is: "Child of Mine, we are in covenant one with the other. I have already given you these things. I have already established them, deposited them, and put them into your account. Now it is up to you, by faith, to draw on what is already deposited there."

You may be trying to work your way to a breakthrough in some area of your life. You may be fasting and praying and trying everything you know how to realize that breakthrough. But stop trying to do it in your own strength. It will be realized only by faith.

Living faith does not have to do works to please God. Living faith does not have to do works to earn a blessing. A person who is walking in a true and living faith does good works, but not to earn God's favor. They do them because of the loving relationship they have developed with God. When we pray, it must not be to impress God, but because we love Him. When we fast, let it be not to earn God's favor, but to draw ever closer to His presence. Everything that we do must be done in response to our covenant God and His great love.

None of our works can add anything to the covenant He has established. There is nothing further to be done. He did it all when He established the covenant through His own sacrifice. It is finished! The covenant is established. Now walk in it and enjoy its blessings.

Use the Word of God in your fight. There is much teaching throughout the Bible regarding covenant, and who we are in Christ. Lay hold of these promises and use them to face down the enemy.

Why do you suppose the Jews in the Middle East fight so furiously for their small patch of land? Why do they care so much? Part of it may be because they need land to exist as a nation and to properly defend themselves. But it is also because they have an understanding of covenant. They have a revelation of the blood covenant that was established between their forefather Abram and Jehovah God. They don't care who it is that is trying to take over that land at the moment. What matters is that Jehovah entered into covenant with their father Abram and that God promised the land would belong to him and to his heirs.

It doesn't matter, therefore, what politicians say. It doesn't matter what agreements are drafted and signed. As far as the Jews are concerned, that land belongs to them — because of the covenant entered into thousands of years ago.

We need that kind of revelation. We need to understand that the covenant between God and us is settled for all time. God does not enter into covenant on a whim. He does not enter into a covenant agreement just because He feels like it. And, once He has made a covenant with someone, He will not break that covenant, for He is faithful to His Word. With the first drop of blood that is spilled, the covenant goes into effect, and it is eternal.

When Sir Henry Morton Stanley conducted his famed search for Dr. David Livingston in Africa, he was confronted by a particularly powerful tribe that tried to hinder him from proceeding. The guide who was with him explained that if he wanted to continue his search, he would have to cut covenant with the chief of that tribe. He wasn't sure what that implied, so he asked. The guide explained that there would be an exchange of gifts, and that blood — Dr. Stanley's as well as the chief's — would have to be shed. Dr. Stanley agreed and they began the process.

Before the blood was shed, they had to exchange gifts. Dr. Stanley was not in good health and took a goat with him everywhere he went for its milk. When the chief said that he wanted that goat, therefore, it was a difficult decision for Stanley to make. If he failed to please the chief and did not successfully cut the covenant, he would not be allowed to continue his search.

In the end, he yielded and gave the goat and, in exchange, he received a tall spear wrapped with copper. To Dr. Stanley, this did not seem like a very impressive gift. After all, what practical good would it be to him? Nevertheless, the covenant was completed, and he departed on his journey.

The very next time his party met someone along the way, a very unusual thing happened. The person they met bowed before Dr. Stanley. He didn't understand this at first, until he was told that the chief had given him the symbol of his own authority. Stanley had been worried about losing a goat, but now he could request a whole herd of goats if he wanted to.

There are some believers who seem to think God is imposing upon them when He asks for their tithes, but this is not an imposition. It is part of our covenant with the Father. He has given us His authority, and all we have to do is lay claim to it in holiness. In return, he has asked for a tenth of our increase. In this way, He is saying to us, "Give Me a little of your goat's milk, and I will give you the symbol of My authority. Wherever you go, men will know that the power of Jehovah is behind you."

Dr. Stanley's goat became the property of the chief, and Sir Henry could not ask for it to be returned. To do so would have been a violation of the covenant.

Abram's giving of the tithe established tithing as the token of covenant, and after Abram had presented his gift, the Lord could legally say, "That tithe belongs to Me."

Some believers may say, "I don't have to tithe if I don't want to." Fine! That's your choice. You don't have to be in covenant with God if you don't want to be. But don't expect to be able to grasp the rod of His authority, or to have some guarantee from God that all the promised blessing will be yours. If you are unwilling to pay God's price, don't expect to receive the benefits of His covenant.

God's blessing upon Abram's life was great. For example, when Abram parted company with his nephew Lot, he gave him first choice of the land before them. Lot took the better land for himself, leaving Abram with the stony ground. Because of the covenant Abram had with Jehovah, however, his stony ground turned out to be the most fruitful. Abram was in covenant with God, and God was legally bound to bless him. So Abram could not fail.

There is one more important step to establishing a covenant. When two men agreed to enter into covenant, they also changed their names. Part of the name of the one man would be made a part of the other's name. This happened with Abram:

And Abram fell on his face: and God talked with him, saying, As for me, behold, my covenant is

with thee, and thou shalt be a father of many na-
tions. Neither shall thy name any more be called
Abram, but thy name shall be Abraham; for a fa-
ther of many nations have I made thee.

Genesis 17:3-5

What was added to Abram's name is much more significant than two simple letters. "Ah" in Hebrew is a breathy sound and represents the very breath of God. So wherever Abraham went, from that day forth, his very name was a reminder of his covenant with God.

God extended this benefit to Sarai as well:

And God said unto Abraham, As for Sarai thy
wife, thou shalt not call her name Sarai, but Sarah
shall her name be. Genesis 17:15

Sarai means "princess," in a relational or affectionate way, and that's not a bad name. God, however, gave her an even better name. Now she was no longer simply a princess but a princess of God and a princess over everything God had. She had been a princess in her relationship with Abram and what Abram had to that point, but when she came into covenant relationship with Jehovah, her territory or area of reigning began to expand. When you are in covenant with God, you actually become a joint heir with Christ:

The Spirit itself beareth witness with our spirit, that we are the children of God: And if children, then heirs; heirs of God, and joint-heirs with Christ; if so be that we suffer with him, that we may be also glorified together. Romans 8:16-17

This being *"glorified together"* is not to be limited to your activities within the walls of your home or church; it is to follow you anywhere and everywhere you go. Abraham was blessed so that he would be a blessing to others, an instrument of blessing to the whole Earth. Even so, we are not blessed of God just so that we can sit back and enjoy His blessing. We are to take this blessing and use it for others:

And he said unto them, Go ye into all the world, and preach the gospel to every creature.
Mark 16:15

But as truly as I live, all the earth shall be filled with the glory of the LORD. Numbers 14:21

The glory of the Lord is not to be simply grasped and held to oneself. It is meant to fill the whole Earth! And who will fill the Earth with God's glory, if not His covenant people?

When you come into right standing with God, you step into a whole new position. Sarai and Abram became Sarah and Abraham. The breath of God became intertwined with their names, and that changed everything. The Bible doesn't say, "By faith Abram ..."; it says, *"By faith Abraham ...."* In the same way, Jacob's descendants did not become the Jacobites. They were known as Israelites, since Israel was the covenant name between God and Jacob.

According to John's Revelation, those who overcome will receive a new name, but we must let it be known here and now that we are changed people. We have taken on the name of our Redeemer, Christ, and are become "Christians." Do those around you see you only as a member of the family? Do they know you only as someone who does a particular job? Or do they know that you are a Christian, that you have the covenant name that sets you apart as being in relationship with God?

You will never execute the authority you have in God until you know where you stand with Him. If you are wondering why certain things are not happening in your life, perhaps you should look to your heart. Are you trying to hold on to your goat's milk, when God is trying to give you His staff of authority? You must give up that goat if you are to be victorious in the land.

Dr. Stanley wanted to hold on to his goat and her milk. He said, "This is what will keep me alive."

But the chief was saying, "There is something in this copper-wrapped stick that will do something very special for you. You have no idea what it will accomplish for you. Take it, in faith." We must do the same.

After the covenant between God and Abraham was agreed upon, it was sealed by circumcision:

This is my covenant, which ye shall keep, between me and you and thy seed after thee; Every man child among you shall be circumcised. And ye shall circumcise the flesh of your foreskin; and it shall be a token of the covenant betwixt me and you. And he that is eight days old shall be circumcised among you, every man child in your generations, he that is born in the house, or bought with money of any stranger, which is not of thy seed.

Genesis 17:10-12

The continuing token of the covenant was circumcision, which, of course, involved the shedding of blood. Circumcision was to represent a necessary renewal of the covenant for each descendant. Every time circumcision was performed in the households of Israel, the participants were saying, "Our family renews the covenant that was established between God and our Father Abraham."

Our symbols of covenant, which we renew regularly, are found in the Communion service. Every time we partake of the elements of the communion, we are publicly acknowledging the covenant relationship of which we are a part, and we are symbolically partaking of the sacrifice that was offered to establish the covenant.

As Abraham fought to protect his sacrifice from desecration, we must do the same:

> *Wherefore whosoever shall eat this bread, and drink this cup of the Lord, unworthily, shall be guilty of the body and blood of the Lord. But let a man examine himself, and so let him eat of that bread, and drink of that cup. For he that eateth and drinketh unworthily, eateth and drinketh damnation to himself, not discerning the Lord's body.*   1 Corinthians 11:27-29

Communion is a holy sacrament, a perpetual reminder of our covenant with God. We are to fight the scavengers that would attempt to eat our sacrifice and examine our hearts, lest we be found to partake in an unworthy manner.

And what of circumcision today? God has determined for New Testament time *"the circumcision of the heart"*:

> *And the LORD thy God will circumcise thine heart, and the heart of thy seed, to love the LORD thy God with all thine heart, and with all thy soul, that thou mayest live.*   Deuteronomy 30:6

> *But he is a Jew, which is one inwardly; and circumcision is that of the heart, in the spirit, and*

not in the letter; whose praise is not of men, but of God.   Romans 2:29

Our hearts are to be circumcised so that we love the Lord and walk in repentance and holiness. Sinfulness, selfishness and disobedience must be cut away.

When we think of our covenant with God, we usually look at only one side of it. We are interested in the blessings we receive from Him, but a covenant is a two-way agreement. It is not only about what we get; it also involves what we are required to give in return. Abraham was severely tested:

And it came to pass after these things, that God did tempt [test] Abraham, and said unto him, Abraham: and he said, Behold, here I am. And he said, Take now thy son, thine only son Isaac, whom thou lovest, and get thee into the land of Moriah; and offer him there for a burnt offering upon one of the mountains which I will tell thee of. And Abraham rose up early in the morning, and saddled his ass, and took two of his young men with him, and Isaac his son, and clave the wood for the burnt offering, and rose up, and went unto the place of which God had told him.

Genesis 22:1-3

There is no biblical indication that Abraham ever argued with God about this trial he faced. He simply got up early the next morning and set about to obey the word of the Lord. He did not complain or lament his lot. In fact, he didn't even say, "Well, here I go to lay down all my desires and to sacrifice all the promises of God to me. Here I go, to do the hardest thing I've ever done, and I wish I didn't have to." What he did say is enlightening:

> *And Abraham said unto his young men, Abide ye here with the ass; and I and the lad will go yonder and worship, and come again to you.*
>
> Genesis 22:5

They were going *"to worship."*

We know the end of the story. We understand that Isaac was spared, and that God, in a beautiful picture of mercy and sacrifice, showed Abraham a ram to sacrifice in place of his son. But understand this: it is very easy for us, when we come into covenant, to say, "God, I claim this part of Your virtue, authority, benefits and blessings," but what happens when God asks you for your Isaac? What happens when God says, "Will you do for Me what I am already willing to do for you?"

The Church today faces the serious problem of living among a grasping, consuming generation. One of the oft-heard indictments against this generation is that we are consuming everything and that we are not willing to put anything back into the Earth or back into society for the generations that will follow. Whether this indictment is totally accurate or not I will leave for the philosophers to debate. I will say this concerning the Church in this generation: we want what we want, when we want it, and the way we want it. The sad part of this is that if you don't like what you are hearing in one church, you can always find another where they will preach what you want to hear. There is always another church, another conference, another book, another teaching. There is always someone willing to tell people that they can live in ways that directly contradict the clear teaching of the Scriptures. There are always those who will tell people that it doesn't make any difference how they live or what they do. But it does.

Most of us are quick to make demands on God. Oh, we don't call them that. Usually they're "prayer requests." They go something like this:

"Lord God, save this one."
"Lord God, deliver that one."
"Lord, I need a new car."
"Lord, I want this."
"Lord, I need that."
"Lord, help me with this."

We ask God for some hard things sometimes, but what happens when God begins to ask us for some hard things? Are you willing to go to your Mount Moriah with your Isaac, to take that which is more valuable to you than anything else in life, and say, "Lord I lay this on the altar; I give it back to You"? This is not an easy thing to do. It was not easy for Abraham, and it will not be easy for you either.

What is your Isaac? Is it a talent or a gifting? Is it a job? Is it security in some form or another? Only you can know what your Isaac is. Whatever it is, are you willing to lay it down and give it to the Lord? Are you willing to allow it to be bathed in the fires of sacrifice?

There are no guarantees. Sometimes the Lord will give us back what we have offered, as He did with Abraham, and sometimes He won't. Sometimes that which we thought was so precious, so golden, is burned as hay in the fire once we have laid it upon the altar.

When you have laid your desires upon the altar and allowed God to deal with them as He will, however, you will see the blessing of Abraham come to pass in your life. God will be able to say, "Now I can trust you. Now I know what kind of respect you have for Me." And He will multiply you and prosper you as He did Abraham. This blessing will not come through the sweat of your brow, it will not come through your travail, and it will not come through your suffering. It will only come forth as a fruit of your blood covenant with the living God.

Hear Him say to you today, *"When I see the blood, I will pass over you."*

Part II:

The Virtues of the Blood

CHAPTER FIVE

THE PRECIOUS BLOOD

Forasmuch as ye know that ye were not redeemed
with corruptible things, as silver and gold, from
your vain conversation received by tradition from
your fathers; But with THE PRECIOUS BLOOD
of Christ, as of a lamb without blemish and with-
out spot: Who verily was foreordained before the
foundation of the world, but was manifest in these
last times for you, Who by him do believe in God,
that raised him up from the dead, and gave him
glory; that your faith and hope might be in God.

1 Peter 1:18-21

The blood of Christ is precious. The Apostle Peter, inspired by the Holy Ghost, wrote of it, and
believers of all ages have sung of it. We were not
redeemed by the standards of man or by religious
traditions, but by the blood of the Lamb, Christ Jesus.
That which redeems us is not just blood, but *"the
precious blood."* In other words, the blood is costly
or valuable.

Some Old Testament sacrifices were considered
to be precious. They had great value or were pur-

chased at great price. Sometimes the cost was in quantity. During the first Passover, celebrated in Egypt, every family was to sacrifice a lamb. Each lamb, it is estimated, was for the redemption of some ten people. More than one hundred and sixty thousand lambs, therefore, were sacrificed on that one day alone, or enough to protect about two and a half million people who made up the nation in exile. That was a valuable sacrifice.

During the reign of King Solomon, the annual celebration of Passover required some four hundred thousand lambs, enough to cover the four to five million Jewish people then living. During the time of Jesus, a quarter of a million lambs were needed for sacrifice. That was a valuable sacrifice.

These lambs were never inferior ones that could be purchased at a reduced price. They were the best of the best:

> *Your lamb shall be without blemish, a male of the first year: ye shall take it out from the sheep, or from the goats.* Exodus 12:5

Each lamb was precious, and massive numbers of them were required to atone for the entire nation. Therefore, sacrificing to God was an expensive proposition for the people of Israel.

Sacrifices were not only required at Passover, of course, and other types of animals were involved.

The Jewish people had many and varied sacrifices. On one very special occasion, when the Tabernacle was being moved to its new home in Solomon's Temple in Jerusalem, the people made so many sacrifices that it was later remembered they *"could not be told nor numbered for multitude"*:

> *Also king Solomon, and all the congregation of Israel that were assembled unto him before the ark, sacrificed sheep and oxen, which could not be told nor numbered for multitude.*   2 Chronicles 5:6

Even more sacrifices were offerered once they reached the Temple. The list found in the biblical record seems to go on forever. That was a costly sacrifice.

When the Temple was later rebuilt, another celebration of joy and expensive sacrifices was recorded:

> *And [they] offered at the dedication of this house of God an hundred bullocks, two hundred rams, four hundred lambs; and for a sin offering for all Israel, twelve he goats, according to the number of the tribes of Israel.*   Ezra 6:17

Sometimes value is not in quantity, but in quality. Some things that take a lot of time to produce or that are produced by especially skilled craftsmen are considered to be valuable. One can purchase a mass-produced set of bedroom furniture fairly economically these days. If it doesn't concern you that many other people may have the exact same furniture or that the quality of the materials and workmanship may not be the best, that's fine. You get what you pay for.

Such furniture, however, cannot be compared with a hand-crafted piece created by a master woodworker. This furniture may not be larger or heavier, but it takes weeks or months for a skilled and experienced craftsman to produce it, while the other furniture pours off some assembly line. Obviously, the hand-crafted piece is more valuable, and most of us would be very proud to own it. It represents a great investment of time, effort and skill, a one-of-a-kind piece.

Distance or availability sometimes determines the value of something. Goods imported from far countries may cost much more because they must be transported. If they are created by a foreign craftsman who has skills not found locally, those goods can be of even more value.

There are many different factors to consider in the evaluation of anything, but however you look at it, the blood of Jesus is *"precious."* It is rare; it took thousands of years to prepare it; and it came to us from a very great distance.

The preciousness or costliness of Old Testament sacrifices was determined by both quantity and quality, but those sacrifices pale in comparison to the sacrifice required in the New Testament. Nothing would suffice except the blood of the Lamb of God, the rarest of the rare.

The blood that redeems us took much time to prepare. Many thousands of years passed between the time man fell into sin and the time of the coming of the Redeemer.

When Adam and Eve rebelled against God and ate of the tree of the knowledge of good and evil, sin entered into the world, and the heart of man became corrupted. A serious wall of separation went up between God and man. But God had a plan even then. He said to the serpent who had been the tool of man's rebellion:

And I will put enmity between thee and the woman, and between thy seed and her seed; it shall bruise thy head, and thou shalt bruise his heel.

Genesis 3:15

A plan developed in the heart of God. A Messiah would come to Earth and would crush the head of the enemy. In the process, Satan would *"bruise His heel."* Christ would suffer on our behalf.

So thousands of years before Christ came to Earth, God had preordained the work His Son would perform. It took time to develop just the right circumstances and situations conducive to God's plan.

Some nations and some kings had to be removed and other nations and other kings had to be raised up. Events had to be molded to suit God's purposes. Then, and only then, *"in the fullness of time,"* Christ was born:

> But when the fulness of the time was come, God sent forth his Son, made of a woman, made under the law, To redeem them that were under the law, that we might receive the adoption of sons.
>
> Galatians 4:4-5

Every detail of Christ's coming was foreordained of the Father. He set the time, the place, and the circumstances so that all would work to His glory. Then everything happened just as the Master Artist had planned it.

The preparation of it all had taken many centuries. It was promised in the time of Adam and came about only in the time of Christ. Just as a valuable piece of furniture takes time — to contemplate, create and produce — so the precious plan of salvation — brought about through the valuable, precious, costly blood of the Lamb — took time to be made ready.

The blood that flowed through the veins of Jesus was more than rare; it was unique! No blood like it has ever flowed through the veins of any other human being. Christ's blood was not of corruptible seed, created by sinful men. It was created by the Holy Ghost.

The Father wonderfully and marvelously hand-crafted the earthly form of the Son of the Living God. No one like Jesus had ever been born or walked the Earth. No one had ever possessed a mind like His. No one had ever possessed a heart like His, or a spiritual insight like His. Christ was not mass-produced; He was One of a kind and He was sent into the world to die for our redemption.

We were all born of corruptible seed, but Jesus was born of the seed of the Holy Ghost. One drop of His blood is more valuable than all the blood that was shed on all the Old Testament altars combined. Because of the rarity and the purity of His blood, because of the preciousness of it, our sin is not only covered; it is actually removed when the blood of Jesus Christ is applied to our hearts.

Valuable because of its rarity, valuable because of the time it took to prepare it, and valuable because of the distance over which it traveled to reach us ... nothing is more valuable than the blood of Jesus. Don't let anyone rob you of that truth.

Jesus did not simply spring up in Bethlehem; He came from the right hand of the Father. He traveled all the way from Heaven to Earth, all the way from glory to dust, to redeem us and make us His own. When Peter called His blood *"precious,"* therefore, he knew what he was talking about. It is costly, rare, hand-crafted, and unique. No one else can match its DNA.

In the case of money, which actually is little more than a piece of printed paper, what gives it value is the reserves behind it or the soundness of the guarantees supporting it. For many years all our money was backed up by gold reserves. Since it was not convenient to carry around huge chunks of gold to pay our bills and fill our gasoline tanks, paper money was developed as a substitute. The paper was not just paper, it was backed by the gold. More recently we have been taken off the gold standard, but when you hold a dollar in your hand, you cling to it and don't want anyone to take it from you. The value is not in the paper or what is printed on it, but what it represents — the authority of the government of the United States of America.

In this respect the blood of Jesus has all of Heaven backing it. Your faith has something of extreme value standing behind it. Each time you minister, each time you pray, each time you exercise your faith, there is something standing behind that spiritual transaction: the blood of Jesus supports everything you do. Your faith does not stand alone, any more than the paper currency we use could stand without something guaranteeing it. It is the blood that activates your faith, and gives it power.

"The precious blood" of Christ covers you, protects

you and heals you. It backs up your faith, enabling you to lay hold of the things of God. Never despise *"the precious blood."*

Hear the Father saying to you today, *"When I see the blood, I will pass over you."*

CHAPTER SIX

THE JUSTIFYING BLOOD

*Being justified freely by his grace through the re-
demption that is in Christ Jesus: Whom God hath
set forth to be a propitiation through faith in HIS
BLOOD, to declare his righteousness for the remission of sins that are past, through the forbear-
ance of God.*   Romans 3:24-25

There was bloodshed at Calvary, where Christ
died for our reconciliation. There was death, too, but
that was not the final result. Christ died so that we
would not have to die. He suffered so that we would
not have to suffer. He took sin upon Himself so that
we could be free of it. This was all part of the Father's
plan. Jesus was *"the Lamb slain from the foundation of
the world,"* and one day all men will worship Him
as such:

*And all that dwell upon the earth shall worship
him, whose names are not written in the book of
life of the Lamb slain from the foundation of the
world.*   Revelation 13:8

Jesus died, but that was not the end of it. After He *"descended,"* He also *"ascended"*:

Wherefore he saith, When he ascended up on high, he led captivity captive, and gave gifts unto men.
Ephesians 4:8

The shedding of blood was part of God's plan from the beginning, and Christ was destined to die *"from the foundation of the world."* This blood, however, was not meant to turn us away or to disgust us; rather, it is to bring life, cleansing, and wholeness.

During the time of Moses, the children of Israel were given many laws that were to be honored in their daily lives, and a significant number of those laws had to do with the shedding of blood. There were laws pertaining to the giving of acceptable sacrifices, laws concerning the celebration of the Passover, laws concerning those who had shed innocent blood, laws forbidding the eating or drinking of blood, and even laws concerning the blood of menstruation and childbirth.

Why were there so many laws concerning blood? I believe the Lord wanted to emphasize the importance of the blood to His people. He instituted these laws so that Israel would not do anything to disrespect or make common the one commodity that would bring God's people back into favor and relationship with Him — the blood. God wanted His people to honor their means of atonement, and that remains His desire until the present day. When you think of blood, think of reconciliation, of favor, and of blessing.

> *For it pleased the Father that in him should all fulness dwell; And, having made peace THROUGH THE BLOOD OF HIS CROSS, by him TO RECONCILE ALL THINGS UNTO HIMSELF; by him, I say, whether they be things in earth, or things in heaven. And you, that were sometime alienated and enemies in your mind by wicked works, yet now hath he reconciled In the body of his flesh through death, to present you holy and unblameable and unreproveable in his sight.*
> Colossians 1:19-22

We are reconciled to the Father by the blood of His Son. This is a fact. There is no longer a separation between us and God. Paul urged every Corinthian to believe for this position of strength in God:

> *We pray you in Christ's stead, be ye reconciled to God.* 2 Corinthians 5:20

Your reconciliation to the Father does not depend on how you might feel at the moment. As we have seen, the enemy of our souls often comes to sow seeds of doubt in our minds. "After you acted in that way," he says, "do you really think God has forgiven you? Well, maybe He did, but surely you don't think His opinion of you is as high as it was before. Of course, He takes you back. He has to. It's just too bad that you'll never again feel the closeness with Him that you enjoyed before." And on and on he goes, accusing you and erroding the foundation of your position in Christ.

Sometimes it is not the devil but our own flesh and our carnal thoughts that are working against us. Discouragement oftentimes is the result of looking to our emotions rather than looking to the Word of God. Even if we do not feel, at times, particularly close to God, that does not mean that He has not done what He said He would do. Our position is established by the blood, not by our feelings.

We can save ourselves from the attacks of emotioanally-based negativivity the enemy brings by reminding our spirit man that our positional relationship is affirmed by the power of the shed blood, not our natural actions, religious works or feelings.

> *Wherefore in all things it behoved him to be made like unto his brethren, that he might be a merciful and faithful high priest in things pertaining to God, to make reconciliation for the sins of the people.*   Hebrews 2:17

It is blood-bought reconciliation that makes possible the expression of the Kingdom of God on Earth and in you. It is only as we walk in fellowship and love with God and with man that those around us realize that something unusual is at work in our lives.

Never forget the justifying blood of our Lord. Justification is one of the most important concepts of the New Testament. We are *"justified freely by His grace."* What does that mean? To be *justified* means "establishing a person justly by acquittal from guilt." If you are justified, you are placed in a different position than that which you occupied before. You are not the same person you used to be, and you are not in the same position you were in before. You have been taken out of the kingdom of darkness and brought into the Kingdom of God. Only the justified are established in God's Kingdom; the justified are acquitted from guilt. You have been brought out of the darkness, so God looks at you and says, "This one is just. He [or she] is among the upright."

Often, one of our fiercest enemies is our yesterdays. People spend so much time and energy meditating on regrets and remorse. Yet no matter how badly you may feel about things you have done in your past and no matter how many good works you do to try to make up for the wrongs you committed, you cannot change your past. The good news is that you can change your present. You can choose to allow God to remove you from a place of guilt, punishment, and judgment and give you entrance into His Kingdom:

> *For the kingdom of God is not meat and drink; but righteousness, and peace, and joy in the Holy Ghost.* Romans 14:17

God's Kingdom is righteousness; it is peace; it is joy. It is not a place for guilt or regrets. God's Kingdom is a place of newness of life. You can enter only if you are justified, and that comes by God's grace and through His blood.

The enemy may come along and say, "What about this sin?" Even if we try to remind God of the wrongs we have done, the Lord will say, "I don't know anything about that. It has been cleansed by the blood." It was taken care of the moment you asked Me for forgiveness. You are in right standing with Me, for you have been acquitted of all wrongdoing. Now be released from the guilt as well, and don't mention that sin to Me ever again."

Some believers want to feel spiritually humble by remembering all the horrible things they did in the past, but this is false humility. It is time to cast your sins into the sea of forgetfulness. We can take Paul as our example in this area. He said:

> *Brethren, I count not myself to have apprehended: but this one thing I do, forgetting those things which are behind, and reaching forth unto those*

things which are before, I press toward the mark for the prize of the high calling of God in Christ Jesus. Let us therefore, as many as be perfect, be thus minded. Philippians 3:13-15

Paul believed that the past should be forgotten, and he personally had quite a lot to forget. He had been guilty of murdering believers, of turning them over to others to be tortured and killed. Before his encounter with Christ, he was brutal, and the worst thing about it was that he did it all in the name of God. A man like that could have very easily been overtaken by remorse. He could have very easily wallowed for years in his guilt. Paul, however, chose to accept forgiveness, to accept acquittal from the Lord. He chose justification through the blood of Jesus Christ.

If you are one of those who constantly dwells on the past, please ask God to deliver you. Accept what He has done for you. After all, He has made every provision for your justification. He has translated you from the kingdom of darkness into the Kingdom of His Son. If He calls you just, if He has acquitted you of your guilt, then you can accept His word on the matter, for His Word is true. He wants you to be free of the guilt of the past so that you can go forward and live for Him.

We are justified through the redemptive work of Christ. We have been purchased; we have been released upon receipt of our ransom. Each one of us

had been held hostage to sin and to Satan's kingdom. Satan took mankind hostage at the Fall of
Adam and Eve. Hostages are not in control of their
situation, and this was true of each of us. Man no
longer had the dominion he had been given by God;
he no longer had the authority that had been granted
to him by the Almighty. Satan was in control of his
life.

Our positional justification is a release from the
power, the punishment, and the guilt of sin. We are
established as just by our acquittal from guilt. We
are redeemed — purchased or ransomed — by the
blood of Jesus. Through the continual, ongoing propitiation of the blood, we are made righteous:

> *And be found in him, not having mine own right-
> eousness, which is of the law, but that which is
> through the faith of Christ, the righteousness
> which is of God by faith.* Philippians 3:9

> *But after that the kindness and love of God our
> Saviour toward man appeared, Not by works of
> righteousness which we have done, but according
> to his mercy he saved us, by the washing of re-
> generation, and renewing of the Holy Ghost;
> Which he shed on us abundantly through Jesus
> Christ our Saviour.* Titus 3:4-6

Our righteousness is not our own. Any true righteousness to be found in us is of Christ, and we re-

ceive it by the work of His shed blood. This word righteousness does not have as much to do with position as it does with character. Righteousness is the character or quality of being upright, and God is forming that character in each of us. We are *"saved from wrath through Him"*:

> *Much more then, being now justified by his blood, we shall be saved from wrath through him.*
>
> Romans 5:9

There could be no greater blessing than to know that *"we shall be saved from [the] wrath [of God]."*

We are being delivered daily from sin's dominion. Sin keeps trying to restore its authority in our lives, but if we are saved, we are delivered, and this is a continual deliverance. Satan may try to bring a particular burden back into our lives, or he may try to ensnare us under a specific yoke of sin that has always caused our problems. But we are no longer bound to live under sin, and we can walk in the daily deliverance that God has provided for us. By His blood we have been released from sin. Praise God!

Paul declared to the Romans:

> *For sin shall not have dominion over you: for ye are not under the law, but under grace.*
>
> Romans 6:14

You need no longer live in your yesterdays. Don't

listen to the lying deceptions of the enemy. Refuse the guilt for sins that have been dealt with by the blood of the Lamb. It is only when you listen to the lies of the enemy that you can be brought back under the dominion of a particular sin. A deceiving spirit may say to you, "You think you've changed so much, you think you've grown in God, but you're not one bit different than you were ten years ago."

Refuse such lies immediately and completely. You *are* different. The blood doesn't touch anyone without changing them forever. You can have confidence that God will complete the work He has begun in you:

> *Being confident of this very thing, that he which hath begun a good work in you will perform it until the day of Jesus Christ.* Philippians 1:6

God will continually perform His work in you, as you allow Him to wash you in His blood. You may have a battle, and you may have a trial, but if you have the remission of sin, then you have been released from the guilt of sin, the punishment of sin, and the judgment of sin. As a believer, you are reconciled and justified, you have been acquitted of guilt, you are being delivered daily from sin and you are living in a blood-purchased position with Christ.

Hear the Lord's voice today saying to you, *"When I see the blood, I will pass over you."*

CHAPTER SEVEN

THE ATONING BLOOD

For the life of the flesh is in THE BLOOD: and I have given it to you upon the altar to make an atonement for your souls: for it is THE BLOOD that maketh an atonement for the soul.

Leviticus 17:11

Since the first sin, since the first bite of that forbidden fruit, atonement has been a crucial concept in God's dealings with man. The word atonement has come to mean different things to different people. When the Bible uses the word, it means "to cover, to pacify, or to placate." In the Old Testament, the concept of atonement was that of "a covering of the blood for the purpose of pacifying or placating a wrathful God."

God has a right to be angry. He created a paradise for man to live in, and the thanks He got was man insisting on doing his "own thing." God is angered by sin. He is not like a child who throws a temper tantrum because he can't get his own way, but God knows that when we obey Satan and not our Creator, we are being robbed of the very best

He has provided for us. That makes Him angry, but His is a righteous indignation.

It wasn't God who broke the relationship with Adam and Eve. He came down that morning to walk and talk with them just as before, but He found them hiding from Him in shame. It was sin that broke the relationship, and it happened because man chose to side with the serpent and not with God. I would be angry too.

There is a serious lack of appreciation these days in the Church for the consequences of sin. Many Christians seem to think that their sin is just a natural part of their character that God accepts. When they display wrong attitudes and commit sinful deeds, they view them as not really being "all that bad." "After all," they sometimes say, "some people are doing much worse things." The idea of walking uprightly or living a holy lifestyle seems to have become an outdated notion in some circles, but this should not be. God expects better of us.

Sin wreaks havoc on your life, destroying your morals, your health, your integrity, your finances and your relationships. Many people have found themselves so totally destroyed in one or even all these areas of their lives that it has caused them to look up to God and seek His help. Satan unintentionally drove them right into the arms of a loving God.

Sin begins in the spirit, but it is a spiritual cancer

that, if left unchecked, will take over every part of our lives and leave us helpless and devastated. Sin doesn't merely destroy your peace of mind; it severely affects your physical world. Many have been left scarred, bruised, and abused because of sin. If you look into their faces, you can see the marks of a cruel taskmaster and the great anguish of spirit his rule has caused.

The sad part about the sin in the lives of believers is that it is not caused by the dominion of Satan, but by the choices of the flesh. Many Christians seem to have forgotten how to resist temptation and die to self.

This is a serious matter because sin has such terrible consequences. Before Adam sinned, he had dominion over the whole Earth and everything in it. That dominion was given to him by God. When he sinned, however, Adam yielded to Satan's temptation, and Satan took advantage of that yielding to illegally take up a position of authority over him. That rule has continued until the present day. Sin dominates the Earth. This is a very different place than God created it to be, and man is a very different creature than God created him to be. Sin changes everything.

In Old Testament times, because of the waywardness of the people, sacrifice became a regular part of daily life. At least once a year sin offerings were given so that the worshipers could maintain a proper relationship with a holy God. The blood of the animals that were slain in those times was not powerful enough to do anything more than cover past sin. It did nothing for sins yet to be committed. It was not in the least bit eternal. The writer to the Hebrews expounded on this:

> *For the law having a shadow of good things to come, and not the very image of the things, can never with those sacrifices which they offered year by year continually make the comers thereunto perfect. For then would they not have ceased to be offered? because that the worshippers once purged should have had no more conscience of sins. But in those sacrifices there is a remembrance again made of sins every year. For it is not possible that the blood of bulls and of goats should take away sins.* Hebrews 10:1-4

Under the Law, there was no lasting freedom from sin, no way to continually walk *"in newness of life."* The sacrifices of the Old Testament bore witness to the fact that the fellowship between God and man had been broken and were a provision for man's forgiveness, but their affects were only temporary. *"The blood of bulls and of goats"* had no power to change the sinner. Something more powerful was clearly needed.

Something more was always part of God's plan.

He had not designed a way to simply cover man's sin, but had decreed the eventual coming of a Savior, a Redeemer, to Earth. Rather than simply appease God's anger and cover over the sins of man, God had a plan that would restore man to the estate from which he had fallen. He would bring man back to the place of power and authority he had lost in the garden. Indeed, He would restore to man the very image and likeness of the Divine. He would raise up children, a people, for Himself, and He would accomplish all this through the death of Christ and His perfect and complete sacrifice. That one offering was sufficient:

> *And every priest standeth daily ministering and offering oftentimes the same sacrifices, which can never take away sins: But this man, after he had offered one sacrifice for sins for ever, sat down on the right hand of God; From henceforth expecting till his enemies be made his footstool. For by one offering he hath perfected for ever them that are sanctified.* Hebrews 10:11-14

"The blood of bulls and of goats" could cover sin, but the blood of Jesus broke its power and offered us true atonement, true redemption, and true restoration. The Old Testament atonement covered, pacified and placated, but the New Testament atonement, through Christ, brings total change. The blood

of Christ doesn't just cover; it *"takes away the sin of the world":*

> *The next day John seeth Jesus coming unto him, and saith, Behold the Lamb of God, which taketh away the sin of the world.*   John 1:29

It was John the Baptist who first recognized the Lamb of God for who He was. The Scriptures said of John that no greater man had ever been born. He had been filled with the Holy Ghost *"from his mother's womb."* Before he was born, he also leaped in his mother's womb when he sensed the presence of Jesus, still in the womb of Mary, his mother's cousin. Now, when he saw Jesus for the first time, there was no question in his mind as to who Jesus really was, and he boldly proclaimed Him to everyone gathered with him that day. He wanted the whole world to know that this was the Lamb and that He would *"take away the sin of the world."*

I find it interesting to note that John did not say that Jesus would "take away our sins." He said that Christ would take away *"the sin of the world."* Theologians have written volumes on this subject, but let us look at it in a very simple way. *"The blood of bulls and of goats"* could bring forgiveness for specific sins, but it could do nothing for the sin question. Jesus was about to do what the sacrifices of the Old Testament could never do. The blood of this Lamb would deal with the very nature of sin. This blood was so rare, so powerful and so supernatural that it could do what the blood of millions of sacrificial animals had not been able to accomplish. This blood would be effective, not only in dealing with individual sins, but also with the sin nature — the root of man's problem.

We are not sinners because we sin; we sin because we are sinners. The sin nature, the fallen nature from Adam, is in us when we are born, and it is passed on from generation to generation. Men are born enslaved to Satan because of the fateful decision of Adam to reject God and obey His enemy. We are no longer in control of things; Satan is in control over us. Paul said of that fateful day:

> *Wherefore, as by one man sin entered into the world, and death by sin; and so death passed upon all men, for that all have sinned:*   Romans 5:12

David wrote that we are *"born in sin"*:

> *Behold, I was shapen in iniquity, and in sin did my mother conceive me.*   Psalm 51:5

Cain was born in sin, Abel was born in sin, Seth was born in sin, Enoch was born in sin, Noah was born in sin, and you and I were born in sin. The sin nature has been part of every human being who has ever walked the face of the Earth since Adam's day. There is only one power that can break the nature of sin in us, and that is the power of the blood of Jesus Christ. The blood of this sacrificial Lamb would do more than simply turn away the wrath of God from His people. It would do more than cover over a few sins. The blood of this sacrificial Lamb, Christ Jesus, would *"take away the sin of the world."*

When the blood of the Lord Jesus Christ is applied to an individual's spirit, something begins to take place deep within them. The yoke of sin that has ruled and reigned over that life begins to be destroyed, and burdens begin to be removed.

Some of you may be thinking, "But I have sinned since I've been saved." I understand that, but you are in a different spiritual position than you were before you were saved. Before you found Christ, you sinned because you were a sinner. That was your nature. You sinned because sin had power over you. Now, however, you no longer *have* to sin. You are no longer out of control, and sin no longer has dominion over you. You are no longer a sinner, for you are a new creation in Christ Jesus, and sin no longer can control you. Sin is now and issue of choice, not control.

Another word the Bible uses to describe our freedom from the power of sin through the blood of Christ is *"remission"*:

The Atoning Blood

And almost all things are by the law purged with blood; and without shedding of blood is no remission. It was therefore necessary that the patterns of things in the heavens should be purified with these; but the heavenly things themselves with better sacrifices than these.   Hebrews 9:22-23

Remission is a word we rarely hear anymore, except in cases of "remission" from deadly diseases. It is a very important word in the Bible, however. It means "release from sin and its guilt and punishment." Release! What a wonderful promise! The blood of Jesus releases you from the hold of sin. It releases you from the guilt and the punishment of sin.

When there is a remission, a release from sin, from guilt, and from the punishment of sin, Satan's power is broken. One of Satan's most lethal weapons is guilt and shame. When you have remission from sin, you render the power of guilt and shame inoperative. The remission of sin through the blood has truly released you.

After He died for us, Jesus presented His blood as the *"ransom"* for our sins. In this way, He has truly set us free from the dominion of sin and of Satan:

For there is one God, and one mediator between God and men, the man Christ Jesus; Who gave himself a ransom for all, to be testified in due time.
1 Timothy 2:5-6

When Jesus spilled His blood, all Heaven rejoiced to see that the full ransom had been paid. There is now absolutely nothing that Satan can do about it. His hold is broken. God is eternally appeased, eternally satisfied. The wrath of God has been turned away from man, and Satan's hold on us has been broken, forever.

You have been redeemed, purchased by the blood of Jesus. You have been released upon receipt of the proper ransom. God has freely, in His unmerited favor toward His people, purchased and released you. The blood of Christ Jesus is our propitiation, or our eternal appeasement, our eternal pacifier, our eternal placator of the wrath of God. It has ransomed us, atoned for us and justified us before God.

Rejoice in your deliverance from sin. Atonement has been made for you, and you may live free of Satan's bondage, through the precious blood of Jesus Christ, God's Son. Hear the Father saying to you today, *"When I see the blood, I will pass over you."*

Chapter Eight

The Restoring Blood

Not by works of righteousness which we have done, but according to his mercy he saved us, by the washing of REGENERATION, AND RE-NEWING of the Holy Ghost; Which he shed on us abundantly through Jesus Christ our Saviour.

Titus 3:5-6

Because there is such a lack of understanding of the blood of Christ in the Church today, many have received erroneous teachings, and, because of it, some do not have the victory they might otherwise enjoy. Many of the teachings that circulate in Christian circles are even dangerous to your spiritual well-being. If you really believed some of them and followed them to their logical ends, you would have to renounce your faith in the blood of Jesus Christ. Obviously, that is a dangerous proposition.

The blood of the Old Testament sacrifices did not have the power of the blood of the Lamb of God, Jesus Christ. The Old Testament blood could not cleanse, deliver or regenerate the individual under its covenant. We are "new creatures" and "born again" because of the blood of Jesus. Old Testament blood had only enough power to cover sin from the eyes of an angry God. Paul's teaching to the Romans can shed some light on this:

> *For what the law could not do, in that it was weak through the flesh, God sending his own Son in the likeness of sinful flesh, and for sin, condemned sin in the flesh.*　　　　Romans 8:3

From the study of the basic doctrines of the Bible we understand that the nature of sin has been passed from one generation to another since Adam.

> *Wherefore, as by one man sin entered into the world, and death by sin; and so death passed upon all men, for that all have sinned:*　　Romans 5:12

> *For as by one man's disobedience [Adam's] many were made sinners, so by the obedience of one shall many be made righteous.*　　　　Romans 5:19

This doctrine reveals to us that we were all born with a corruptible nature, one that will result, no matter who we happen to be by birth, in rebellion against God and His Word. Erroneous teachings on "generational sin" and "generational curses" are based on Old Testament teaching:

The Restoring Blood

Thou shalt not bow down thyself to them, nor serve them: for I the LORD thy God am a jealous God, visiting the iniquity of the fathers upon the children unto the third and fourth generation of them that hate me;   Exodus 20:5

Such scriptures basically teach that we are cursed because of the sin our fathers, grandfathers, or great-grandfather's committed. While it is easy to see how this teaching was released into the Body of Christ, it is not applicable for our dispensation. We are not under the Law, but under the New Testament in Christ's blood. That makes all the difference in the world.

The Law *"was weak through the flesh."* The life of the flesh is in the blood, and the blood that was sacrificed under the Old Testament was not powerful enough to reverse certain parts of the curse. The ability to break a generational curse from a person's life took a greater power, a greater authority, than was available in that dispensation. In the same way the Old Testament atonement was a covering, but the New Testament sacrifice brings redemption and regeneration. The New Testament truth is not a generational curse but: *"If any man be in Christ, he is a new creature."* Since this is so, it really doesn't matter who your natural forefathers were or what they did. It no longer affects you.

The blood of Jesus Christ has a power that supersedes any other force that has ever been released on the face of this Earth. You have entered into the covenant of the blood that brings a blessing to your life and that destroys anything that anyone has done in your generational yesterdays.

Some refuse to believe this. I can only say to them, "If you want to place yourself under someone else's sin and under their curse, that is your choice, but there is freedom for you in Christ if you want it. If you will only access the power of the blood, you can be free from the past."

Nicodemus asked Jesus how he could possibly be born again. His mind was on the physical impossibility of it. Jesus replied, in essence, "That's not what I'm talking about. I'm speaking of a regeneration. I'm speaking of your heavenly Father becoming your true Father."

It is time for us to come back to theological basics. We must understand the blood of Jesus, what it is and what it does for us. Otherwise we will live far short of our privileges. We must refuse to subject ourselves to false interpretations of the Scriptures. Jesus said:

> *And ye shall know the truth, and the truth shall make you free.* John 8:32

God did not set you free so that you could become bound again, so that He could set you free the second time or the third time. You are free. PERIOD! Your very nature has been changed. There is no one else to blame for your sin now. Jesus paid the price for you, and there are no more excuses.

The benefit of the blood has given you the dawning of a new day. It has given you a brand new start. *"Old things are passed away."* They are dead and gone. How glorious! What a blessing!

There is another side to this truth: our responsibility. It is time for us to take responsibility for our own actions and stop blaming our forefathers for the way we have been acting. Stop blaming the person who hurt you fifteen years ago. Stop blaming your present actions on what someone did to you when you were twelve. Stop looking to your childhood, or to the abuse you have suffered, or to what happened in a previous relationship. Stop prying into the lives of your great-grandparents or your parents, looking for generational sins.

You are a new creation, and God has cancelled every curse meant for your life. He considers that matter resolved, so why do you keep digging it up again? If you still need to be healed of something, ask God to heal you by His blood, by the stripes that Jesus suffered for your sake. But please stop blaming everything on the past and on others in your family. All of that has been erased. It's gone. Let it go.

The Old Testament sacrifices could not bring

about this type of change. The Old Covenant did not afford regeneration or deal with the sin nature, but the New Covenant does. Rest in it. There is complete cleansing and renewal in the New Testament for all who will believe and receive. Remember, you are born again because of the blood.

Why was idolatry such an abomination to God? It was not simply that the people were worshipping other "gods." There was more to it than that. When Israel fell into idolatry, the sacrificial system fell apart, and there were virtually no sacrifices being offered. No blood was being spilled to cover the sins that were being committed and, as a result, the anger of God was not being held back. Because the blood of the Old Testament sacrifices could not bring the restoration of spiritual life, the new birth, when the Old Testament atonement was lifted, it exposed the sinful, rebellious nature which, in that dispensation, had not yet been reversed.

Suppose you had an old table, full of scratches and water stains. You could put a beautiful, clean tablecloth on that table and set it with costly china, lovely silverware and candelabras, you could place a centerpiece of fresh flowers in the center of it, and when your guests arrived, they might exclaim, "Oh, what a lovely table you have set for us!" But you would know the truth. Under all the trappings, that table would, in reality, still be ugly. Although it might look good for the moment because it was covered and adorned, that would not make it a beautiful table.

This is exactly what happened with the Old Testament shedding of blood. It provided a covering for sin, but it failed to change the nature of the people. It was only a momentary fix.

Under the New Covenant, things are entirely different. You are no longer an old, marred vessel. All your scratches, stains and discolorations have been removed by the blood of the Lamb. You have been cleansed and restored!

When I was a child, my mother had a coffee table that she loved. Over time it became discolored and scratched, and one day it disappeared from the house. It had not been discarded, for my mother knew that under all the scratches and stains was some lovely wood that could be restored with proper supervision. She had taken it to a skilled worker who stripped it, buffed out the nicks and scars and then refinished it. When they brought that table back into the house, it was more beautiful than it had ever been. It had been totally cleansed and restored. That is what God does in the New Covenant — by Christ's blood.

I had a mentor who enjoyed restoring old cars. Once, when he had gotten a 1949 Cadillac, his wife, his daughter and I looked at it together. We all agreed that it was "nothing but a wreck."

The man wasn't discouraged by our assessment

of his purchase. "Just wait until I get done with it," he said. "You'll see."

Over the next several months this man worked many hours on his car. He ordered the exact cashmere fabric that had been on the original seats. He replaced the windshield. He found original tires. He tore the engine apart and completely rebuilt it. He had to wait weeks, and even months, for some of the parts he had ordered, but gradually he rebuilt, resurfaced and refinished the whole car. Finally, he had it repainted in its original color.

One day he said to me, "Tim, come here. I want to show you something." I walked with him out to where the car was parked, and I could sense his excitement. He had every reason to feel proud of his accomplishments, for that car sat there gleaming in the sunlight, looking very much like a brand new vehicle. As I looked it over, I could barely believe that it was the same car. He had done an amazing job of restoration, and the finished product was a beautiful sight to behold.

That man had a choice. He could have taken a tarp and covered that old, badly worn car to hide its ugliness. But he chose, instead, to see its value and to do the long and arduous task of cleansing and restoration. Something that had become very ugly with time had now been restored to its original glory.

God saw you in your broken-down, ruined condition, and He reached out to you. Only He could picture the beauty that might be made of your life. He gathered you to Himself, and with a single drop of His blood made you a born-again one, a restored model. You are not an old, scarred table or a broken-down jalopy. You are not under anyone's curse. No devils can inhabit you, for now you are a new creature in Christ Jesus. *"Old things are passed away,"* and *"all things are become new."* If we believe the blood does anything less than this, we insult God.

The blood applied to our lives continues its work after our initial regeneration. If you still have something from your past that bothers you and you feel guilty about it, by faith apply the blood in that area of your life, but then let go of it. God has released you, and you should receive His release. There is no need for you to carry around a lot of excess baggage. Jesus has already paid the price to free you from the past. Why keep going over things you did years ago? Christ has forgotten them all.

We see these principles at work in the life of Peter. He was one of the original disciples of Christ, but he had a sin nature that could not be properly dealt with before Calvary. Peter's life was a serious dichotomy. He was the man who preached in the street at Pentecost, but he was also the man who denied Jesus three times. He was the man who cut off the ear of the high priest's servant, and he was the man who was willing to be crucified upside down for the sake of Christ. Something was very different about this man after Christ died; he was walking in the power of the blood.

Because Christ died for us, nothing of the past need be held over us or need hinder our spiritual progress. No past failure, past hurt or any generational sin has power over us. These are all taken away by the blood of the Lamb.

Just as we were reconciled *"by the death of [God's] Son,"* we *"shall be saved by his life"*:

> For if, when we were enemies, we were reconciled to God by the death of his Son, much more, being reconciled, we shall be saved by his life.
>
> Romans 5:10

Stop looking for some attachment to the powers of darkness. Stop looking to the failures of the past. Forget what people did to you years ago. This is a new day.

It is true that we were once kidnapped and living in darkness. God didn't create us to live that way, but the devil had grabbed hold of our lives, snatching us from the place where God originally intended us to be. Satan was holding us for ransom, but Jesus said, "I will pay the price to buy My people back," and He did.

Now He says, "Satan, you must give them up. They are not yours anymore, for I have paid their ransom." The devil, therefore, no longer has a legal claim on you, generational or otherwise.

Christians who believe that the devil still has some sort of hold on them don't understand the power of the blood. Satan is not "the dark side of God," as some claim. He can do nothing that God does not allow him to do. Why would God go through all that He did to purchase you, only to let the devil have his way with you?

You are God's prized possession and are more valuable to Him than houses, cattle or lands. When the devil came to tempt Jesus in the wilderness, he told Him He could have *all the kingdoms of this world*," if only He would bow down and worship him. Jesus answered:

> *Get thee hence, Satan: for it is written, Thou shalt worship the Lord thy God, and him only shalt thou serve.* Matthew 4:10

What was Jesus really saying? He was saying, "I don't care about those other kingdoms. I have come to serve My Father, and I will do that by saving *that which was lost*." I am not looking for worldly kingdoms, for riches or for possessions. I already own all that. What I'm looking for are the men and women you have kidnapped. You took them out of the place My Father had for them, but I will buy every one of them back with My blood." That is just what He did. You have been redeemed, and you are God's treasured possession.

Most of us are careful with our possessions. We lock our houses and our cars, and we use alarm systems to protect them from intruders. These are expensive items and we don't want anything to happen to them. How much more will God guard and protect those for whom the Son paid the highest possible price?

We can expect to have peace and health and blessing. Don't expect any more curses and demon control of your life. God did not save you, heal you, and deliver you to let you remain under some curse.

Embrace all that God has done for you by the power of the blood. Your past has been forgiven and you are cleansed and released. You are in no way responsible for the sins of your forefathers. Relax in the love of your Father and hear Him say to you today, *"When I see the blood, I will pass over you."*

CHAPTER NINE

THE PROTECTING BLOOD

Then Moses called for all the elders of Israel, and said unto them, Draw out and take you a lamb according to your families, and kill the passover. And ye shall take a bunch of hyssop, and dip it in THE BLOOD that is in the basin, and strike the lintel and the two side posts with THE BLOOD that is in the basin; and none of you shall go out at the door of his house until the morning. For the LORD will pass through to smite the Egyptians; and when he seeth THE BLOOD upon the lintel, and on the two side posts, the LORD will pass over the door, and will not suffer the destroyer to come in unto your houses to smite you. And ye shall observe this thing for an ordinance to thee and to thy sons for ever. Exodus 12:21-24

Some who read this passage get a wrong impression about God, as a killer, a destroyer, and He is not. Satan is the destroyer, not God. In the book of Job we find an interesting story about Satan that helps us clarify our thinking in this regard.

One day, the story goes, the sons of God had presented themselves before Him, and Satan also came in before the throne. When God asked Satan where he had been, he answered that he had been wandering over the Earth.

God asked him, "Have you noticed My servant Job? There is no one like him. He is a righteous man who fears Me and who casts aside evil at every turn."

Satan wasn't so sure:

> *Then Satan answered the LORD, and said, Doth Job fear God for nought? Hast not thou made an hedge about him, and about his house, and about all that he hath on every side?*   Job 1:9-10

As the account continues, we find the Lord giving Satan permission to tempt Job for a season. Satan argued that there was a hedge around Job and that he could not breach it, and he begged God to take it down. God agreed to remove it temporarily, but assured the devil that Job still would not turn from Him. "I know Job," God insisted, "he is a truly righteous man."

There is a great revelation in this passage for those who will receive it. Satan has a severely restricted and restrained authority. He is not nearly as big as many think he is nor as big as he would like to make us believe he is. There are so many restraints on him right now that it would amaze us if we could see just how many chains he is dragging around.

The Protecting Blood

On this occasion, the Lord loosed Satan, but only for a specific length of time and for a specific purpose. Beyond that, Satan could not go. He was powerless without God's specific permission.

So when God stepped onto the scene that first Passover night, He was not the destroyer; Satan was. God simply released Satan to destroy the firstborn of any household that was not protected by the blood, and Satan was limited to the specific orders God gave him.

Satan had not been able to touch Job because of the divine hedge that was around him, and when we have favor with God, Satan cannot get at us either. Why should we fear him? He cannot do anything God does not specifically permit him to do.

It was this *"angel of the bottomless pit,"* this *"destroyer"* who moved throughout Egypt on the night of the first Passover. It was he who killed the first-born, by sovereign release. Why hadn't he killed the firstborn before that? Because God was showing mercy toward the Egyptians and had not yet released the devil to destroy them. If Satan could have killed the firstborn of Egypt anytime he wanted, the firstborn would have been dead a lot sooner, for he is intent on killing.

God gave specific instructions to the children of Israel the night he released the death angel upon Egypt. They were to take a lamb from their flocks, kill it, and prepare the Passover meal. They were to sprinkle some of its blood on the doorposts and lintel (the framework) of the door and to remain indoors for the night, under the protection of that blood. As the destroyer moved through Egypt, he had to ask permission from God for each step he took.

"Can I go in here?" he asked.

"I don't see any blood," God answered. "Go on in."

"How about that house? Can I go in there?" asked Satan.

"I don't see the blood," God replied. "Go ahead."

If the blood had been applied to any Egyptian door, the death angel would not have been allowed to enter it. In every house where there was no sign of protection to be found, the destroyer was allowed to enter that night, and the firstborn of the household died.

When Satan came to the land of Goshen, where the people of Israel lived, he asked, "Can I go in there?"

"No!" the Lord said, "I see the blood."

God then positioned Himself at the door of every blood-marked house and would not allow the destroyer to enter. No matter how much the accuser spoke against those who were within, no matter how much his nature as thief and murderer made him want to get at those who were reaching toward liberty from Egypt and a trip toward the Promised Land, God would not allow him to pass. The blood prevented it.

Most people have felt the term Passover had to do with God passing over a household, like a plane might fly over a rooftop. However, the term Passover, in this context, had to do with an encompassing of God's power and presence around the households of those who loved Him. That presence was not drawn by the righteousness of the people, but by the application of the blood of the Passover.

God took personal responsibility for every house that had the sign of the blood. He personally stood in front of each door, and the enemy had to back away. He knew that he could not get through Jehovah. No doubt he presented every accusation he could against the children of Israel and explained in detail why they were not worthy to be spared, but his accusations carried no weight. God wasn't looking at people or their failures or their unworthiness. He was looking at the blood.

When the blood of Christ is applied to your life, to the doorposts of your heart, the enemy can rant and rave all he wants, but he cannot come in. The blood of the Lamb, when applied to the heart and life of a believer, provides protection from the enemy, his accusations and all his normally-deadly activities.

The devil will surely still accuse you. He may say,

"But, Lord, he isn't as spiritual as he looks. Let me tell You what he did."

God will answer, "I know everything this child of Mine has done, but he is covered by the blood of Christ, and I will deal with His sins Myself. I don't need your help, Satan. This is a family matter. The Holy Ghost will deal with it. He will not condemn My children, but He will convict them. He will take them into the Word and, in the end, they will laugh at you because they will overcome you by *'the word of their testimony.'* "

In the past, you may have walked in fear and intimidation of the enemy, but there is a power that is stronger than any the enemy has at his disposal — the power of the blood. The blood has the power to protect you from every enemy.

Paul wrote to the Ephesians:

Neither give place to the devil.   Ephesians 4:27

This may be a small verse, but it speaks volumes. We are not to give any position of influence to the devil. We are not to listen to his lies. We are not to go looking for him. We are not to magnify him. If you are a blood-bought child of the Lord God, then demons have no rights, authority, or dominion over you.

The children of Israel were to apply the blood to their houses, and they were also told to stay in their houses that night. They were to remain inside their dwellings, securely hidden away from the destroyer. As we dwell and abide in the Lord, He is our Hiding Place, our Rock of Refuge. If you want to be protected from the attack of the enemy, then stay in the house.

If you insist on trying to live by your own philosophy, then you need to be aware that there is no safety in the philosophies of man. That is not a safe house. There is no guaranteed protection in the forms and rituals of religion. Your only protection is to stay within the covenants God has established with His blood.

If you are a child of Abraham by faith, then every covenant promise of God is yours. Those promises are the bricks that build your spiritual house. The blood is the mortar that joins them into strong walls that cannot be torn down. That is the house in which you may safely dwell without fear. *"God has not given us the spirit of fear"* (2 Timothy 1:7).

There is another account in the Bible in which someone was told to remain in a house and to use the sign of the blood for protection from destruction. It is found in the second chapter of Joshua.

Two men of Israel had been sent into Jericho to spy out the land. Rahab, a local resident who had come to fear the Lord, hid the spies from her king. In exchange for her silence concerning them, Rahab was promised protection when Israel would come to take the land, but there were two conditions:

Behold, when we come into the land, thou shalt bind this line of scarlet thread in the window which thou didst let us down by: and thou shalt bring thy father, and thy mother, and thy brethren, and all thy father's household, home unto thee. And it shall be, that whosoever shall go out of the doors of thy house into the street, his blood shall be upon his head, and we will be guiltless: and whosoever shall be with thee in the house, his blood shall be on our head, if any hand be upon him.

Joshua 2:18-19

The two spies did not yet know what the battle plan would be for taking the city. Joshua didn't even know it yet, for God had not yet given it to him. God had a plan for Rahab.

When the attack came, the army would not simply knock down the gates, kill the people, and burn the city. They were not strong enough militarily to do that. Instead, they would march around the city silently for seven days, and on the seventh day, the walls would suddenly begin to crumble and fall.

When the day of victory came, the two spies suddenly thought of Rahab. Her house had been high on the wall of the city. They had told her to stay inside her house, but now all the houses were crashing to the ground. They had told the other men of the army to look for the scarlet thread, but now it wasn't up to the army to decide who lived and who died. And who could find a scarlet thread in all that mess?

The two men were probably in a state of panic. "How could we have done this to the woman?" they asked. "She harbored us from our enemies, and we promised her, by the Lord, that no harm would come to her. We promised her that she would be safe."

Then something supernatural happened. God looked down out of Heaven and saw that scarlet thread, that symbol of the blood. He said, "I see the blood. No matter what is falling around that house, the blood will protect it." The walls came crashing down on all sides, but when the dust settled there was a lone column standing in the wall and a woman could be seen standing unhurt at the window. In that window was a scarlet thread. Rahab was safe because of the blood. This is a protecting blood, and the Lord Jehovah repeats to us today, *"When I see the blood, I will pass over you."*

Part III:

How to Achieve the Benefits of the Blood

CHAPTER TEN

THE AUTHORITY OF THE BLOOD

Behold, I give unto you POWER ... OVER ALL THE POWER OF THE ENEMY: and nothing shall by any means hurt you. Luke 10:19

If you have ever taken time to read through old hymn books, you may have noticed in many of them an emphasis on the blood. Many of our oldest and most beloved hymns deal with the sacrifice that bought our salvation. This was a reality that believers thought about, preached about and sang about. It was not just an abstract idea to them. They knew its importance.

We don't see that much anymore, especially in our modern hymns. Many of the songs that are being written today are wonderful, and they exalt the Lord. They place a healthy emphasis on worship and praise, and we can't complain about that, but as good as these themes are, there is still something missing in our hymns when we fail to reverence the blood of Christ.

I would go so far as to say that there is a subtle deception over the Church robbing us of the very best God has for us. Something is very wrong when we attempt to ignore the power of the blood.

If we ignore the power of the blood, we are forced to find something else to replace it, and what might that be? It seems to me that most people want to believe that in some way our good works, our efforts at righteous living, will cause us to change and to become the person we desire to be. It is time to face facts. We *"are by nature the children of wrath"*:

> *Among whom also we all had our conversation in times past in the lusts of our flesh, fulfilling the desires of the flesh and of the mind; and were by nature the children of wrath, even as others.*
>
> Ephesians 2:3

We were born rebellious and disobedient. Because of the offenses of Adam, sin and death came upon us all. It is only through the obedience of Christ in giving His life for us that we can have a reprieve.

That reprieve does not come simply because Jesus lived on this Earth. It does not come because He was born in human form. It comes because He offered Himself as a sacrifice for sins, and God demanded that blood sacrifice.

When we think of Calvary, we often try to do so in terms that erase the gruesomeness of what happened there. Rather than what Christ suffered there, we choose to think of what He purchased for us through His sacrifice. Calvary represents salvation, healing and deliverance. We forget, however, that in order to purchase our salvation and our healing and our deliverance Jesus suffered unspeakably. His blood was shed as He was beaten beyond recognition. He bled from a great variety of wounds, and He was stripped naked and shamed. It was not a pretty scene.

When the Old Testament sacrifices were offered in the Temple, the Brazen Altar was not a pleasant sight to behold either. It was not a place you would take your children for a pleasure outing. The place reeked of sweat, of blood, of fear, and of death.

Why would God allow the sacrifice for sins to be done in such a gruesome way, both on the Old Testament altars and at Calvary? I believe that He wanted us to constantly remember how gruesome sin, with all its consequences, really is. Sin is not just an issue of making bad decisions. It is not a matter of rethinking your position. It is an insidious nature inherent in every man and woman because of the Fall, and the only way to get rid of it is through the blood of Jesus. You cannot cast out the nature of sin; you cannot exorcise it. The only thing that can conquer the nature of sin is the blood of Christ.

When His blood is applied to the doorposts of your spiritual house, the gateway to your heart, the access to your spirit, you literally draw the encompassing presence of the Spirit of God around your life. When the blood of the Lamb is applied to the doorpost of your house, the glory of God Himself comes into your life. Jesus said:

> *Behold, I stand at the door, and knock: if any man hear my voice, and open the door, I will come in to him, and will sup with him, and he with me.*
>
> Revelation 3:20

Jesus is standing at the doorway of your heart and spirit. He wants to come in and sup with you. He wants to have communion with you. You cannot share that communion, however, unless and until you properly discern His body and His blood. He is saying to you, "I am standing at the point of access to your eternal spirit, and I am knocking, seeking entrance. If you will open your spirit to Me, I will come in and have fellowship with you, and you with Me" — all because of the shed blood.

If you want to vanquish the enemy and have total victory in your life, two things need to be functioning: *"the word of [your] testimony"* and *"the blood of the Lamb."* The blood must be applied first because the covenant does not become ratified until you have accepted the need for cleansing in the blood. God doesn't owe you the promises of the Bible; they are His gift to you, and you must receive them in the way that pleases Him.

Think about some of those precious promises:

But as many as received him, to them gave he power to become the sons of God, even to them that believe on his name. John 1:12

Behold, what manner of love the Father hath bestowed upon us, that we should be called the sons of God. 1 John 3:1

Ask, and it shall be given you; seek, and ye shall find; knock, and it shall be opened unto you.
Matthew 7:7

And I will give unto thee the keys of the kingdom of heaven. Matthew 16:19

Greater is he that is in you, than he that is in the world. 1 John 4:4

If God be for us, who can be against us?
Romans 8:31

No weapon that is formed against thee shall prosper. Isaiah 54:17

And there are many, many others just like these. These are great promises, and anyone has the right to read them, but the only people who can claim them as their own and appropriate them for their daily lives are those who are covered with the blood of Christ. God is not obligated to release the contents of the Book to just anyone. Without the authority of the blood at work in your life, you have no right to access His promises. The Bible is powerful, and there is a promise in the Bible for any problem we might face, but the stark reality is that you cannot access those promises without the blood.

Those who have used ATMs, automated teller machines, know that you must have a PIN, a personal identification number, to access the machine. Once I wanted to make a withdrawal from my account after banking hours, so I went to the ATM machine. I had my card with me, so I inserted it into the machine, and the machine recognized it. Next the machine asked me for my PIN, and I suddenly realized that I hadn't used it enough to remember it by heart. My mind was blank. The money was in the bank, and the ATM was ready to process my request, but I could not remember the access code.

I tried some numbers that came to mind, thinking I might just stumble onto the PIN, but none of those numbers worked. I even tried talking to the machine, begging it to give me my money, but it refused to respond. I prayed and asked the Holy Ghost to bring the number to my remembrance, and even that didn't work. In the end I had to walk away, frustrated because I could not get to the cash I needed.

The treasures of God must be accessed in the same

way. There is an eternity of wealth within the pages of the Bible, just waiting for you to claim it. You cannot access your account, however, without a PIN. That number is the same for each one of us: B-L-O-O-D. That's the only way you can come into the blessings and the promises of God. You cannot do it without the blood.

At some point the blood of Jesus must penetrate your spirit. The door of your spirit must be open so that communion can truly take place. Only then will Jesus sup with you, and you with Him. This communion can only take place if you have properly discerned and have a true revelation of the body and the blood of Christ.

When we participate in what we now call the Communion Service, we take the cup in our hands, and we take a portion of the bread, but even the act of taking communion can be meaningless for millions. If you don't have the blood of Jesus applied to your heart, going through the motions won't do anything for you. You will still be denied access to true communion with God.

The only way to overcome the enemy is through the blood, for this is the key to spiritual authority. Fasting and prayer is not the most important key. Spiritual warfare is not the most important key. Perfected praise is not the most important key. If you expect to win over your enemy, you must overcome him by *"the blood of the Lamb."*

Many of us hope to gain victory through some-one else's faith, and we travel long distances to receive the laying on of hands of the great ministers of our age. That is all well and good, but you will never have a complete victory through someone else's prayers. You may become better positioned, your ears may be unstopped a bit, and you may feel better after receiving the prayers and ministry of others. But you will never have an overcoming walk with God until the blood has been properly applied to your life. At some point you must come to the sure knowledge that the blood was shed for you. You must have a heart understanding that the blood accesses the Book. And you must know that the Scriptures, which are real and true, can and will be yours as you are properly aligned to Christ through His sacrifice.

The blood of Jesus is strong enough to purge us of our sins, and it is strong enough to protect you from any danger. The world around us can be a frightening place. The news is full of horrifying reports each day. We need a sense of protection in our lives, and the blood can provide it.

Our enemy is vividly described by Peter:

> *Be sober, be vigilant; because your adversary the devil, as a roaring lion, walketh about, seeking whom he may devour.* 1 Peter 5:8

He is seeking *"whom he may devour."* That little

word *"may"* implies a crucial question: who may the devil devour?

At Passover, the destroyer was allowed to take the firstborn of every house in Egypt unprotected by blood. He had access to the Hebrews as well as to the Egyptians, but he could only touch those households that were unprotected. He could not simply take whomever he wanted. The blood was a protection to those who believed the word of the Lord through Moses and who applied the blood to their houses.

We must decide: either the blood of Christ is as mighty as the Word of God says it is, or it is not; either we can look to the blood for protection, or we cannot; either the Word of the Lord is true, or it is not.

As the temple of the Holy Ghost and as members of the Body of Christ we have the right to exercise the authority of the blood of Jesus. The Apostle Paul said:

> *What? know ye not that your body is the temple of the Holy Ghost which is in you, which ye have of God, and ye are not your own? For ye are bought with a price: therefore glorify God in your body, and in your spirit, which are God's.*
> 1 Corinthians 6:19-20

We were *"bought with a price."* Our bodies are *"the*

temple of the Holy Ghost." We belong to God. So why would God give us into the hands of the devil?

This is currently an important issue in the Church. There are some who teach that believers can be possessed by demons, and many other doctrines have developed from that teaching. In order to believe such things, however, one must renounce the blood. Either this blood has the power the Word of God says it does, or it does not, and the Bible is not true. If the devil can access your body as he wills, then you are not protected by the blood. This is a serious issue because it calls into question your position as one of the redeemed. If Satan can enter you any time he wants, you have a serious problem, and that problem is not just temporary. This is an issue of eternity, a potentially soul-damning problem.

If you have been born again, then you are no longer your own. You have been *"bought with a price."* I don't belong to myself. My flesh is no longer *my* flesh, and my body is no longer *my* body. I belong to God, and He has some responsibilities in this transaction. One of His responsibilities is to protect me from the enemy who is looking for someone to devour.

God has given me the blood as my protection, my shield. The devil may go around all he wants seeking *"whom he may devour,"* but I am not an entree for him. My body, my mind, my soul, my spirit — all belong to God. God's Spirit bears witness with mine that I am His son.

Many Christians today live under judgments or curses that, in reality, have no part in them. They have believed the words of others and have drawn calamity to themselves from which the blood could have spared them. Oppression, depression, anger, sin ... God's people are suffering many things that they need not suffer. We are learning to live with many things we have no business living with. Either the blood of Jesus holds the cure, or it doesn't. We must be convinced in our hearts once and for all.

Many lies that are being cast about are receiving a ready audience, and these lies are quickly permeating the Church. We must be careful, or we will become fodder for the devil. If we play with strange fire, we will get burned. The Word of God is emphatic in this regard:

> *Behold, I give unto you power ... over all the power of the enemy: and nothing shall by any means hurt you.* Luke 10:19

"Power ... over all the power of the enemy ..." is that not absolute? Is that not clear enough for us? *"Nothing shall be any means hurt you"*: could God say it any more emphatically than that? What else do we need to hear?

It doesn't matter if you are facing a demon of lust or a demon of envy. It doesn't matter where that demon came from. It doesn't matter whether that demon is a heavyweight, a middleweight or a lightweight. You have, through the blood, power over *"all the power of the enemy,"* and that is more than enough.

I hate to see Christians being terrorized. Some believers are so traumatized that they are convinced they will never be happy. Some believe they can never overcome the enemy in a particular area in their lives. Some are convinced that they will always have to live with a certain difficulty. That arouses a righteous indignation in my spirit. Either the blood works, or it doesn't work. If it doesn't, then we might as well pack up and go home. We might as well not waste our time in church if God will not do what His Word declares that He will.

If the blood works as God says it will, if it brings protection from the enemy and freedom from the bondage of sin in our lives, then that changes everything. Although the circumstances of our lives may not always be easy, and although our every problem may not be immediately resolved, we can walk in hope and in freedom from bondage because of the blood of Jesus shed on Calvary for us. Accept this truth by faith, like little children.

Paul admonished the Church:

> *But let a man examine himself, and so let him eat of that bread, and drink of that cup. For he that*

cateth and drinketh unworthily, eateth and drinketh damnation to himself, not discerning the Lord's body. For this cause many are weak and sickly among you, and many sleep.

1 Corinthians 11:28-30

Wake up, Church! It is time to get well! It is time to give ourselves to the Lord and His sacrifice, and to regain a revelation of the power of His blood and the liberty it brings us. Start exercising the authority of the blood and stop expecting to be overruled by Satan's power.

As I have faithfully preached the power of the blood in recent years, I have seen the principle of reconciliation and restoration at work in the lives of many people.

Wake up Christians! Either you are born again, or you're not. You are either mentally, physically, and spiritually the property of God, or you're not. God didn't just save your spirit; He saved all of you.

We are not just metaphysical spirit beings floating through space and time. We are earthen vessels, made of flesh, but filled with God's glory. We have emotions and thoughts like any other human being, but God has done a work of restoration, renewal and redemption in us through the blood of the Lamb, and we are not captive to Satan's whims. We have the authority of the blood of Jesus.

God did not destine you to fail, but to win. When

the devil begins to speak failure into your life, cast that thought aside, bringing it into captivity. Your house, your being, is no place for the enemy. Be free through the sacrifice of Christ at Calvary. You have the authority of the blood, and God is saying to you today, *"When I see the blood, I will pass over you."*

CHAPTER ELEVEN

THE VOICE OF THE BLOOD

And the LORD said unto Cain, Where is Abel thy brother? And he said, I know not: Am I my brother's keeper? And he said, What hast thou done? THE VOICE OF THY BROTHER'S BLOOD crieth unto me from the ground.

Genesis 4:9-10

Abel's blood sacrifice was accepted, while Cain's grain offering was rejected, and Cain's refusal to accept correction or to repent led to his murdering his brother and living thereafter as an outcast on the Earth. Something else very interesting is said of this event in the Scriptures: *"the voice"* of Abel's blood was crying out to God from the ground.

Some men may get by with their crimes on Earth. After all, our justice system is far from perfect. Not all those who deserve to be jailed end up there, and not everyone who commits a crime is punished. There is, however, a much better and higher judicial system awaiting us all. In the Courtroom of Heaven, truth will prevail. At the Great White Throne Judgment, nothing will be hidden and, in the meantime, the blood of the innocent cries out from the ground.

This fact should startle many, for when God is the Judge, there is no defense. He knows the truth, and He swiftly executes judgment and performs justice. It can be no other way.

The statement of scripture that the blood speaks is not easy for us to understand with our finite minds. We think of blood as being inanimate, but the Scriptures declare that it actually cries out, calling for vengeance and for justice.

The Bible is a supernatural Book. It is not a psychological treatise or a philosophical volume; it is a spiritual book. If you are ever to embrace it, you must do so by faith. You must allow opportunity for the Holy Spirit to take you to a level on which you understand that God's ways are not your ways, and His thoughts are not your thoughts. God's ways and His thoughts are so much higher than our own.

I could try to scientifically convince you that what the Word of God says is true, but you probably never would experience salvation in that way. Because the Book was written under the inspiration of the Holy Ghost, it has to be received by the spirit of revelation. It must be allowed to permeate the inner man of the spirit.

If you are to be able to lay hold of this idea of the speaking of the blood, you must think in spiritual terms. You cannot simply accept it philosophically;

neither can you enter into it psychologically or theo-
logically. You must spiritually absorb it.

I don't understand how people can be anointed
with oil for healing and be healed. It is hard for me
to understand how someone can live a vile life, come
to the Lord and repent of their sins on their death-
bed, and be able to eternally make Heaven their
home. There are many things I must accept by faith.
I don't even really understand how they get that picture on my television screen, but I can watch it and
enjoy it anyway. If you keep approaching the Word
from an intellectual viewpoint, you will never tap
into what you need to get your breakthrough.

Somehow Abel's blood spoke, whether we understand it or not. His blood cried out to the Father.
And his was not the only blood that cried out:

> But ye are come unto mount Sion, and unto the
> city of the living God, the heavenly Jerusalem, and
> to an innumerable company of angels, To the gen-
> eral assembly and church of the firstborn, which
> are written in heaven, and to God the Judge of
> all, and to the spirits of just men made perfect,
> And to Jesus the mediator of the new covenant,
> and to the blood of sprinkling, that speaketh bet-
> ter things than that of Abel.
>
> Hebrews 12:22-24

Christ's blood also speaks, and it speaks *"better*

things than that of Abel." Here we find a bridge built between the Old and New Covenants. Under the Old Covenant, God heard the voice cry out. Under the New Covenant, the blood was crying out again, but it spoke of *"better things."*

Abel's blood, shed because of hatred, jealousy, and murder, cried out for vengeance. It was crying out for judgment. Under the Old Covenant when blood was shed through violence, that blood immediately cried out for justice and vengeance. The blood that was spilled on Calvary, however, the blood that flowed from the Lord Jesus, was not crying out to God for judgment or vengeance. It was crying out to the Father to show mercy to the world. It was crying out to God to bring forgiveness, salvation, and redemption to the people. That blood spoke of something *"better."*

When you go before the Father in prayer, the only thing that gives you voice in the throne room is the blood. You cannot come to God boldly in your own self-righteousness or because of the good works you have done. You cannot say to Him, "I come confidently to the throne because I prayed forty hours this week," or "I come boldly to the throne because I was on a forty-day fast," or "I come boldly because I am a moral person." When we come to the throne of God it is only through the veil of the flesh of the Lord Jesus Christ.

Every time you claim a promise in the Name of

the Lord Jesus, it is the blood that gives that promise voice. When you come before the Lord, you can declare, "I am not here in my own strength. I am not here because of anything I have done. I am here only because of the shed blood of Jesus." His blood pleads for you. The blood cries out for you, not against you. The throne of grace is a place where judgment is turned to mercy, but the only way that happens is through the blood of the Lamb.

What does it mean to "plead the blood"? It is our acknowledgment of our reliance upon the work of Christ in His atoning sacrifice. We have looked into the Word to see what that sacrifice has accomplished for the Church, and for us as individual believers. But there is another aspect to the pleading of the blood: this truth that the blood has a voice with God. It has a pleading capacity before the Father. Jesus could not plead your case as the Mediator if His blood had not been shed. Every aspect of our walk with God hinges on His shed blood. He could not plead your case without it. You would not be out of the darkness without it. You would not be in a position to be delivered, to be healed, to be blessed, to be filled with joy and peace, if it were not for the blood of the Lamb.

The blood speaks of the mercies of God. As we have seen, it turns aside the wrath of God. Whatever the reasons for God's anger, the blood calms it.

Jesus is the Mediator of the New Covenant. His

blood pleads before the Father on our behalf. God may well have reason to be agitated with you, but the Lord Jesus, as your Attorney, says, "The blood I shed on Calvary pleads this case." That blood He shed two thousand years ago is pleading. It's crying out for mercy. It's crying out for your forgiveness. It's crying out for something *"better."* At Calvary, Christ said, *"Father, forgive them, for they know not what they do!"* He is our Intercessor and His blood cries out for us.

Throughout the Bible, we see the blood symbolically crying out on behalf of God's people. At the Passover, the blood spoke from every doorpost. As the destroyer came threateningly by, the blood sprinkled on the doorposts of the houses of Goshen cried out, "You cannot come through this door, you cannot enter this place," and the destroyer had to pass on.

The blood cried out through the scarlet silken cord of Rahab, and she was saved. A single scarlet thread was not strong enough to hold up a tower, but it was able to touch the heart of God with its cries, and Rahab and her family were spared.

Now, in New Testament time, the blood of Jesus speaks with the voice of a new day, a new dispensation, a new time. It speaks of *"better things"* than the blood that was spilled before it. We now have a High Priest who can be *"touched by the feeling of our infirmities."* We have a High Priest who was *"in all ways tempted as we are, yet without sin."* We have a covenant that does not discriminate against us because we are not born Jewish in the flesh. We have a covenant that says, "By faith you are the seed of Abraham, and therefore Abraham's promises are upon you." Red, brown, yellow, black, or white, Jew or Gentile, bond or free ... there is no discrimination in the New Covenant because it *"speaks of better things"* for all mankind.

The blood provides our continual access to God. In the days of the Old Testament, only the high priest could enter the Holy of Holies, and that only once a year. When he went into the Holy of Holies, he wore a robe hemmed with bells and had a rope tied to one ankle. In the case that he did not survive his meeting with God and died there, others would notice that the bells had fallen silent and could grasp the rope and pull his dead body out of that place.

Thank God it is not like that with us. We can enter into God's presence every day of our lives. We can come before the Lord of Glory *"to find help in the time of trouble,"* to find healing for our lives. And we have that privilege only because Christ's blood speaks of something better than the blood of Old Testament sacrifices.

Christ brought the fulfillment of the Old Testament Levitical system. His blood has fulfilled the works of the Brazen Altar. We have no more need of the Brazen Laver, for it is the Word of God that now cleanses us. The Lampstand is no longer needed, for the Holy Ghost is the Spirit of revelation and of enlightenment to us. We no longer need the Table of Shewbread because we now have the cup of the New Covenant, and Christ's body is our bread. The incense that was upon the Golden Altar spoke of our prayers that ascend continually to the Lord, so we no longer need to burn incense.

Jesus was the fulfillment of the Ark of the Covenant that was made of wood and overlaid with gold. His had come in the form of corruptible flesh, but He was inlaid and overlaid with the glory of God. He was also the pot of manna, for He is the Bread of Life. He was the rod of Aaron that seemed to be dead and yet budded and brought forth new life. The tables of the Law that were kept in the Ark were also fulfilled in the righteousness of Christ Jesus. Truly this is a better day, and truly His blood speaks of *"better things."*

The Book of Hebrews speaks more clearly of this truth:

Which was a figure for the time then present, in which were offered both gifts and sacrifices, that could not make him that did the service perfect, as pertaining to the conscience.

But Christ being come an high priest of good things to come, by a greater and more perfect tabernacle, not made with hands, that is to say, not of this building; Neither by the blood of goats and calves, but by his own blood he entered in once into the holy place, having obtained eternal redemption for us. For if the blood of bulls and of goats, and the ashes of an heifer sprinkling the unclean, sanctifieth to the purifying of the flesh: How much more shall the blood of Christ, who through the eternal Spirit offered himself without spot to God, purge your conscience from dead works to serve the living God?

Hebrews 9:9 and 11-14

A will (or a testament) does not come into effect until the one who has written it has died. The will that Jesus wrote could not be put into effect until His death, and His death required the shedding of His blood.

Notice the phrases: *"as pertaining to the conscience"* and *"purge your conscience."* The blood of Jesus deals with the conscience. There are many definitions of conscience, but the one we need here is "the faculty by which we apprehend the will of God, and which is designed to govern our lives." The voice of the blood speaks to our conscience, our faculty to apprehend the will of God. If we listen, we could avert many of the problems we face on a regular basis.

There is much confusion among us today because people are not being led by their conscience, that faculty that reveals the will of God for our lives. We are too driven by the passions of the flesh, by the lust of the eyes, and by pride, and these things lead to destruction. When Christ's blood is applied to our conscience, our conscience is purged. When the blood is applied, our conscience is delivered from dead works. Things begin to change within us. We no longer simply hear God's will spoken to our conscience, but we also begin to act on it.

God has a lot to say to each one of us, and He is faithful to speak. The problem, usually, is that we are not listening. It takes time to quiet ourselves enough to hear what the Lord would say, and when we do listen, we too often fail to lay hold of what we are hearing by applying it to our lives. If we are willing to cooperate with God, His blood will speak to our consciences, allowing us to know and to carry out His will and purpose in our lives.

The voice of the blood intercedes before the Father, and the voice of the blood speaks to us, as well. What could be more important?

When the blood speaks to our hearts of "better things," we are compelled to look again to the pages of Matthew, Mark, Luke, and John. We are compelled to read again the accounts of the early Church as found in the Book of Acts. We begin to absorb the writings of Paul and Peter and John and James.

Without that impact of the blood of the Lamb, we could spend hours reading the Bible and never find the will of God for our lives in the Scriptures. We would just be reading words. We might understand a philosophical ideal or find a good historical perspective, but if we are to understand the will of God that is designed to govern our lives, it will take time spent in listening to and apprehending the voice of the blood.

If you have you ever felt confused about your purpose, as most of us have at one time or another, if you have ever felt as though you did not know what God wanted you to do with your life, then you can appreciate the value of the voice of the blood of Christ. We each need the revelation of the will of God to govern all aspects of our lives, as individuals and as a Body. God will cause all confusion to lift:

> *For God is not the author of confusion, but of peace, as in all churches of the saints.*
>
> 1 Corinthians 14:33

Elsewhere He has promised:

> *Thou wilt keep him in perfect peace, whose mind is stayed on thee: because he trusteth in thee.*
>
> Isaiah 26:3

He is our Peace, and He brings to us peace and an end to confusion.

God can direct us and order our steps, but we

must realize that our acceptance does not depend upon our good works. Our acceptance is through the blood.

> *He hath made us accepted in the beloved. In whom we have redemption through his blood, the forgiveness of sins, according to the riches of his grace.* Ephesians 1:6-7

You are accepted because of the shed blood of the Lamb. Learn to listen to the voice of that blood. It speaks on your behalf before the Father, and it speaks on His behalf to you.

God is saying to you today, *"When I see the blood, I will pass over you."*

CHAPTER TWELVE

APPLYING THE BLOOD TO YOUR LIFE

And they overcame him by THE BLOOD of the Lamb, and by the word of their testimony; and they loved not their lives unto the death.

Revelation 12:11

"They overcame him ..." What an important phrase! The blood of the Passover lambs brought protection to the children of Israel as the destroyer went throughout Egypt on his fearsome errand against the firstborn of that land. There was more to that protection, however, than just sacrificing a lamb. The sons of Israel were not merely to slay a lamb and thus spill its blood. It was not enough for the blood to be shed. They could have slain as many lambs as they wanted and still have remained defenseless when the destroyer came their way. That blood also had to be applied to the doorposts of the houses if it was to be effective in protecting their homes against the coming death.

This is an important key to your victory as well. Activation of our faith requires the application of the blood of our Passover Lamb, Christ Jesus, to the doorposts of our spiritual houses. As we seek the Lord and plead the blood, we will see the promises of God begin to be worked out in our lives. The application, however, is essential. If there is no application, we can only speak of the benefits, never receive them. It was not the blood alone that brought protection to their lives, but the application of that blood.

The Lord said to them, *"When I see the blood, I will pass over you."* He was not saying that He would do a quick fly-by. He was saying that He would encompass the people with His presence and protect them from the intent of the destroyer. It was the blood that would make the difference. It had to be applied where it was clearly visible.

Concerning our Lamb, the One who shed His blood for us, it is not enough that the blood has already been shed. If that were enough, then every person born since that time would automatically be part of the Church. There would be no need of repentance and of receiving the indwelling Christ. There would be no need of the new birth, since the blood was spilled for all mankind.

We know, however, that we do need these things. It is not enough that the blood was shed. It is not enough that we acknowledge that it was shed. We must apply it, each of us, to his or her own spiritual house, his or her own spirit.

As we apply the blood, changes begin to occur in our lives. Suddenly we notice that we have a Protector. There is Someone standing between us and our enemy. This is what salvation is all about — the application of the blood, the accepting and receiving of Christ's sacrifice and its power in our lives.

As we continue in our Christian walk, we may see areas of our lives that fail to line up with the Word of God. We may begin to hear God directing us to change in certain ways. How, then, do we respond? We apply the blood of Christ. We say, "Yes, Lord, You are right. I do need to change. I know that I cannot do this in my own strength. Please, Lord, be my strength. Change me, Lord, and cause me to be more like Jesus. Wash me with Your blood, and cleanse me from sin."

The same destroyer who devastated the homes of the Egyptians wanted to do the same to the Israelites, but he was prevented from doing so. He has not changed, for he still wants to come against the people of God today. He wants to take over your life. He wants to destroy you — physically, emotionally, spiritually, relationally and financially. He wants to steal your faith, your joy, your life. He wants to kill your walk in God. In fact, that is his total agenda:

The thief cometh not, but for to steal, and to kill, and to destroy. John 10:10

The enemy will do all he can to destroy you and me, but the Lord has said, *"When I see the blood, I will pass over you, encompassing you with My presence. I will not allow the destroyer to strike you down."* The Lord's protection comes when you apply the blood of Jesus to your life.

There are churches today that have no revelation of the blood, and there are entire denominations that have literally ignored its power. Should we wonder, then, that the power of God is not present in those churches? There is no other means found in scripture whereby we may overcome the evil one, and without the revelation of the blood, we cannot really walk in an overcoming faith; we cannot really lay hold of the covenant promises of God.

One way in which we symbolically partake of the blood is through Communion. Paul, in his letter to the church at Corinth, mentioned those who did not have a proper respect for the blood of Christ:

For he that eateth and drinketh unworthily, eateth and drinketh damnation to himself, not discerning the Lord's body. For this cause many are weak and sickly among you, and many sleep.
1 Corinthians 11:29-30

Applying the Blood to Your Life

When men and women fail to respond properly to the Communion table, it must surely be because they lack a revelation of the blood. We can hardly blame the people sitting on our pews, for many preachers no longer want to preach the revelation of the blood. This is a tragic mistake.

Some people are motivated, but they get nothing from God because they are not in a right relationship with Him. Some people are motivated, but they are just like *"sounding brass"* and *"a tinkling cymbal."* They are motived, but I fear that they will not make Heaven their home. They are missing the essence of what the true new creation, born-again relation is all about. If we are new creatures, it is only because Christ died on Calvary for our sins. If we are born again, it is only because He chose to shed His own blood for us. This is not a new and radical message. This is the same age-old story of the cross.

If the Church is ever to become what God has ordained it to be, we must have the glory of God. That glory will never come because of all the things we do, but only because of Christ's atonement. The healing, the blessing, the presence of God all come because of the blood applied to our lives. It is that blood which causes God to reverse the curse. It is that blood which takes us out of darkness and into His marvelous light.

When the Church comes to an understanding of the power of the blood, when believers begin to respect the blood, and when we begin to walk in that revelation, then the breath of the Spirit, the presence of the Lord, will enter the Church in a new way.

It is then that we will see the holiness of God manifested in the people. We have tried to put on holiness from the outside in, but it just doesn't work. We try to be holy through form and ritual, but it must come through an internal change.

Do you long to live a victorious life? Do you long to overcome the enemy, that evil one who would accuse you day and night? Do you long to live free from his taunts? Then lay hold of the revelation of the blood of Jesus. Understanding the blood is pivotal to living the victorious Christian life.

Why the Church as a whole no longer wants to talk about the reconciling blood of Jesus Christ is a mystery to me. Whether we want it or not, we need to be taught the importance of His sacrifice, and we need to come into a biblical understanding of the power of the blood of Jesus in our lives.

Many are declaring that they receive all the promises of the New Testament through their faith, but that is not what Jesus said. At the Last Supper, He told His disciples that the New Testament was *"in [His] blood."* Yes, you need faith, but you would never have been in a position to have faith or exercise it if it had not been for the shedding of Christ's blood. Without that sacrifice, it would be impossible for you to say, "I believe that by His stripes I am healed." It was the shedding of His blood that made this promise available to you.

It is absolutely essential that the Church today grasp this afresh and anew. Satan wants to hinder that revelation from coming fully upon the Church. He doesn't want us to understand that the blood of the Lamb is what bought the promises, that the blood of the Lamb is the voice that speaks in the heavenlies, that the blood of the Lamb is what protects us from the destruction of the enemy, that the blood of the Lamb is what condemns the very stronghold of sin. If the enemy can keep us ignorant of these things, then we shall be destroyed *"for lack of knowlegdge"*:

> *My people are destroyed for lack of knowledge.*
> Hosea 4:6

Just as God breathed His breath into Adam, and man became a living being, so He longs to breathe His life anew into the Church. That is how the Church will be raised into greatness, by walking in the true revelation of the blood of the Lamb. If the blood of Jesus had not been needed to bring man back to the Father, then that blood would never have been shed. But it was needed, and therefore Christ came to Earth. As the songwriter declared:

> *What can wash away your sin?*
> *Nothing but the blood of Jesus.*

We could add:

What can bring protection to your life? Nothing but the blood of Jesus.

What speaks for you in the heavens? Nothing but the blood of Jesus.

What speaks to us of *"greater things"*? Nothing but the blood of Jesus.

What can bring you into a covenant relationship with God? Nothing but the blood of Jesus.

What can cause you to be reconciled with God? Nothing but the blood of Jesus.

What can appease the wrath of an angry God? Nothing but the blood of Jesus.

What brings us remission of sins, the release from sin and its guilt? Nothing but the blood of Jesus?

What can bring us justification, acquittal from guilt? Nothing but the blood of Jesus?

What can ransom our souls from the hands of Satan? Nothing but the blood of Jesus.

What can provide a propitiation of our sins? Nothing but the blood of Jesus.

What can make us righteous in the eyes of God? Nothing but the blood of Jesus.

If you are longing to be free, then you must allow the power of the blood be applied to your life, so that God can impart to you salvation, health, strength, and vision. When He sees the blood, He will pass over you.

And THE BLOOD shall be to you for a token upon the houses where ye are: and WHEN I SEE THE BLOOD, I WILL PASS OVER YOU, and the plague shall not be upon you to destroy you, when I smite the land of Egypt. And this day shall be unto you for a memorial; and ye shall keep it a feast to the LORD throughout your generations; ye shall keep it a feast by an ordinance for ever.

Exodus 12:13-14

Other Books

POSSESSING YOUR PROPHETIC PROMISE

At a time when the church has been blessed by the greatest period of expository teaching of the Word of God than any generation has experienced, at a time when we have more resources available to us then ever before, why do so many of God's people seem to wander for years in the wilderness without ever experiencing a breakthrough into the fullness of what God has promised to them? Why have so many received miraculous provision and protection but still have not scratched the surface of their spiritual potential? It is time to possess our prophetic promises.

But what must we do to cross over the river Jordan and possess our Promised Land? What steps are necessary to dislodge every enemy and take back what is rightfully ours?

As only he can, Dr. Tim Bagwell brings forth the revelation that God has given him to bring YOU to the place of *Possessing Your Prophetic Promise*.

Perfect bound. 168 pages. ISBN 1-885369-12-X   *$9.99*

ASK FOR IT IN YOUR FAVORITE BOOKSTORE

OR CALL:

1-800-9McDOUGAL

- *Notes* -

ABOUT THE AUTHOR

DR. TIM BAGWELL has been acclaimed as a twentieth century prophet and as one of the greatest preachers to ever grace the American platform. He has touched hundreds of thousands of lives since the early 1970s.

His ministry, through evangelistic crusades, conferences and seminars, has taken him across the U.S. and to many other nations of the world, preaching the uncompromised Word of God with signs following. He has ministered in Canada, Haiti, Norway, Holland, Switzerland, the Middle East and Brazil.

Pastors throughout the world solicit his ministry because of its balance of pastoral and evangelistic experience. The churches he ministers in are blessed by the gifts of the Spirit and the bold, uncompromising ministry of the Word.

His book *"Possessing Your Prophetic Promise"* was released in 1995. He and his wife Gayla also released a music album, *Living the Legacy* that same year. In 1996, the first edition of *Empowered for the Call* was released and in 1998, both an updated version of that book and this new book *When I See the Blood* first appeared.

The Bagwells have been married since 1975 and have two sons: Adam and Aaron.

Dr. Bagwell currently serves as senior pastor of The Word of Life Christian Center in the metropolitan Denver, Colorado, area.

Ministry address:

Dr. Tim Bagwell
7498 S. Clarkson
Littleton, Colorado 80122